P9-DER-916

3337

**Mountain View Christian School**
**305 Fleming St.**
**S. Williamsport PA 17702**
**327-9238**

# SAFEGUARDING THE LAND

## Women at Work in Parks, Forests, and Rangelands

by the same author: **Honest Andrew**

# Safeguarding the Land

**Women at Work in Parks, Forests, and Rangelands**

## Gloria Skurzynski

Illustrated with photographs
FOREWORD BY **Cecil D. Andrus**
FORMER SECRETARY OF THE INTERIOR

HARCOURT
BRACE
JOVANOVICH
New York and London

Cover photo: Duane McClure

CREDITS: Craig Nelson, Photographic consultant. Boise Interagency Fire Center, pages 56, 62, 72, 75, 80, 81, 87, 89; Bureau of Land Management, pages 113, 115, map on 135; National Park Service, page 37; Neil Gilchrist, *The Times Standard,* Humboldt Newspapers, Inc., page 131; Janey McDowell, page 52; Duane McClure, page 29; John Reynolds, *The Salt Lake Tribune,* page 44; Gloria Skurzynski, all other photos

Requests for permission to make copies of any part of this work should be mailed to: Permissions, Harcourt Brace Jovanovich, Inc., 757 Third Avenue, New York, New York 10017

Printed in the United States of America

LIBRARY OF CONGRESS CATALOGING IN PUBLICATION DATA

Skurzynski, Gloria.
Safeguarding the land.   Bibliography: p.   Includes index.
SUMMARY: Traces the careers of three women involved in public land management and outlines opportunities for those interested in this field.
   1. Women in conservation of natural resources—United States—Juvenile literature. 2. Conservatioin of natural resources—Vocational guidance—United States—Juvenile literature. 3. United States. National Park Service—Officials and emloyees—Juvenile literature. 4. United States. Forest Service—Officials and employees—Juvenile literature. 5. United States. Bureau of Land Management—Officials and employees—Juvenile literature. [1. Women in conservation of natural resources. 2. Conservation of natural resources—Vocational guidance. 3. Vocational guidance]  I. Title.
S945.S55      333.73′16′02373      80-8805
ISBN 0-15-269956-2      AACR1      ISBN 0-15-269957-0 (pbk.)

B C D E      First edition      B C D E (pbk.)

For the three in this book;
for Serena, Janine, Joan, Alane,
Lauren, Heather, Nancy, and Mary and for
all the other courageous young women
who have accomplished so much

# Contents

# *Foreword*

---

**W**hile I was growing up in the Pacific Northwest, there was no question in my mind that someday I would have a "man's job" in the great outdoors. In time I achieved my boyhood dreams, although the lure of public service eventually brought me to the cities, even to our nation's capital.

As I matured, and as our nation has matured, it has become evermore apparent that the definitions of "man's work" and "woman's work" which existed during my youth are no longer valid. This became especially meaningful to me while raising three daughters. "Why," I began to ask myself, "shouldn't they have the opportunity to use their energies and talents in any field they wish to pursue?"

The exclusion of women from many jobs—especially in the field of natural resources management and conservation—was not only unfair but was a terrible waste of human resources. During this past decade, tremendous progress has been made in opening up jobs and positions for women in fields that previously were the domain of men only.

When I became Secretary of the Interior in 1977, I made special efforts to place women in various positions of high responsibility previously reserved for males. But I made it clear that these women were appointed because they possessed the intellect and dedication to do the job, not just because they were women.

One problem that the resources management agencies have encountered is finding women with the training required for professional positions. Many of the general schedule positions in the Department of the Interior are classified in the sciences and engineering series. Many others require technical or professional specialties. Until recent years, there were few incentives for women to get this education because there were no jobs open to them.

As this book makes clear, there are now opportunities for women to get into the field as park rangers and in other jobs as resource managers. These are not jobs for the fainthearted of either sex. These jobs demand intelligence and dedication.

Here we have the personal stories of three young women who were determined to become "rangers." We can experience some of the obstacles they encountered and surmounted.

Young people—male or female—who think they might have an interest in working in resources management will find this an interesting and useful appraisal of the joys and hazards of working in the field. Others who are concerned with resources management also will find this both informative and entertaining reading.

Times have changed since I was a young boy preparing for a "man's job"—and obviously for the better.

Cecil D. Andrus
Former SECRETARY OF THE INTERIOR

# SAFEGUARDING THE LAND

## Women at Work in Parks, Forests, and Rangelands

# Introduction

## A NEW FORCE IN THE RESOURCE FIELD

*I*f you haven't been to one of America's national parks lately, you probably think of a park ranger as a friendly, helpful young man in a neat uniform. Picture a forest ranger and you see a man protecting forests from fire, with a little help from Smokey Bear. Until a decade ago these images would have been correct, because most ranger jobs went to men.

Now picture a woman in a park ranger's uniform. She kneels on a wilderness path giving first aid to a girl who's been horribly mauled by a grizzly bear, using all her skill to save the girl's life.

Another woman walks through a national forest in Montana, counting baby fir trees that had been planted by the hundreds the summer before, and feeling concern because so many of the seedlings had died from drought.

A third young woman clips grasses and shrubs on a high mountain ridge in southern Utah, weighing them on a hand

MARY JANE McDOWELL
Park Ranger

KAREN ECKELS
Wildfire Specialist

JAN KNIGHT
Range Conservationist

scale. Her work will insure that a free-roaming herd of buffalo has enough to eat.

Within the past few years, women have begun to do these jobs, which were once considered "man's work." They're still so new at it that the phrases "the first woman who . . ." or "the only woman to . . ." occur again and again in this book about three young women in our federal resource agencies—the National Park Service, the U.S. Forest Service, and the Bureau of Land Management.

Asked why women were slow to find acceptance in these agencies, one official explains, "It's not that people were trying to keep women out of certain nontraditional roles. It's just that it never occurred to them that any woman would be interested or would have the background."

When women finally started working in these fields, they performed very well, the official says, adding, "I think we're probably beyond the first flush of 'My God, a woman couldn't do that!' to the point where more women are being accepted without great hue and cry."

This book looks at the roles of women in resource jobs and examines the jobs themselves, whether they're performed by men or women. It also describes the agencies—their histories, the responsibilities of each one, and the conflicts that arise when the public balks at some of their policies. But mostly it's about the lives and work of three women, Mary Jane McDowell, Karen Eckels, and Jan Knight.

# Janey McDowell

## THE TRAINING OF A RANGER

*M*ore than 2 million acres of the world's most spectacular scenery fill Janey McDowell's backyard. It's a land of geysers, hot pools, and mud volcanoes. Of pelicans, grizzlies, and moose; tall lodgepole pines, and tiny algae. Janey is a ranger in Yellowstone National Park.

Growing up in Little Rock, Arkansas, Mary Jane McDowell played with paper dolls and played the flute in the school band, never dreaming that she would one day exchange her band uniform for the uniform of a park ranger. She wore her thick dark hair in a ponytail, had braces on her teeth, and grew to be the tallest girl in her class.

The McDowell family had fun together, but they were not outdoor people. They didn't go camping or fishing, preferring to spend vacations visiting relatives or lounging on a beach. Janey's first experience with the out-of-doors came after her sophomore year at Memphis State University in Tennessee.

To earn money for tuition, Janey accepted a summer job as a Girl Scout camp counselor, and a whole new world opened up to her. Hiking with the girls under the hot Tennessee sky, teaching songs and games beneath sheltering trees, Janey felt a sense of space and of closeness to nature that she'd never known before. How satisfying it would be, she thought, if she could find a career that would let her work in the open, let her live with trees and stars and sky.

Back at college, she changed her major to park administration. During her senior year she took the Government Entrance Examination and applied for a job with the National Park Service. Janey realized that competition for the National Park jobs was always fierce, but she wasn't aware that at about that time, Congress had granted money for the hiring of ninety new Park Service employees. When word reached her in September, Janey was elated. The Park Service wanted to hire her. She was going to be a park ranger.

During three months of training at Grand Canyon National Park, Janey and forty other ranger-trainees had to decide whether they wanted to enter the field of interpretation or protection within the Park Service. Protection rangers safeguard both parks and visitors. They fight fires, police the areas, and rescue lost or injured hikers.

Interpretive rangers take visitors on nature walks and give talks that make the park's history and environment come alive. When the trainees were evaluated near the end of the three months, a counselor told Janey that she could do well in either field, although not too many women went into protection. Perhaps that challenge helped Janey make up her mind. She chose protection work.

Her training was not yet over. The Park Service had begun to realize that many city dwellers, especially urban children, have no opportunity to travel to the red and orange cliffs of Zion National Park, to the towering snowfields of Glacier

National Park, or the virgin hardwood forests of the Great Smoky mountains. The National Park Service was created for the benefit of all Americans, and those who live on crowded inner-city streets have a need, perhaps a greater need than others, for outdoor education and recreation. To help fill this need, Janey was stationed for four weeks at George Williams College north of Chicago.

Boys and girls from the Chicago area were brought for a week's stay to a Park Service site on Lake Geneva, where Janey and other rangers took them stargazing at night. In the daytime, they might tour a city park. Janey would blindfold the sixth graders, take them by the hand, and lead them through trees. "Concentrate on all your other senses," she'd tell them. "What do you hear—a bird singing? Can you smell the pines? How does the earth feel beneath your feet?"

That was the summer of 1973. After the Chicago experience, Janey's classmates were split up and sent to six different cities to receive further urban-training while they waited for permanent assignments. The wait stretched to five months. In Washington, D.C., Janey and nine others performed a number of Park Service jobs, anxious to be sent to a field area where they could "really do ranger work," in Janey's case, the protection work she had chosen but had not yet had a chance to practice.

From the six cities the classmates kept in touch by telephone, eager to hear where each had been assigned to permanent duty. Every trainee was allowed to list a preference for a particular area of the country, and most had chosen the West. Obviously not all of them would be able to work in the West, and tension mounted as the wait for assignments went on.

Meanwhile, every trainee's file was being studied at Park Service headquarters for qualifications and preferences, for instructors' recommendations, and training records. One after another, Janey's classmates learned of their placements; still she didn't know where she would go. In Washington one of the rangers had a big map on his apartment wall. As they heard about each classmate's assignment, Janey and the others stuck pins in the map to show where that person had been sent.

She was one of the final ones to be told. The phone call came at last, nine months after she'd joined the Park Service. Janey's first ranger assignment was at Mesa Verde National Park in Colorado.

## MESA VERDE

*T*he chief ranger didn't know what to do with her. Not only was Janey the first woman ranger ever assigned to Mesa Verde, but she was in the protection division! How could a woman handle search-and-rescue missions, fight fires, and enforce laws in an area where ancient Indian dwellings lean against sheer-faced cliffs or perch beneath sweeping overhangs of sandstone, where some of the crumbling ruins can be reached only by steep ladders? The chief ranger was not at all certain that Janey could.

Days and weeks passed as she waited for duties to be assigned to her, but nothing happened. She was a real ranger in an important national park, but she might have been another tourist for all the notice her supervisor gave her. The scenery was splendid, 52,000 acres of desert and mountain set near the corner where Utah, Colorado, New Mexico, and

Arizona meet. After far too many hours spent watching purple sunsets, exploring Indian ruins, and settling her belongings into the house the park provided her, Janey wanted to go to work.

But the chief ranger continued to ignore her, and the permanent male rangers were skeptical about her ability. After a while Janey's confidence in herself became shaky.

"I had to have somebody believe that I was going to be all right and that I was going to do a good job," Janey recalls, "but the others just didn't think I could do it. And I let it happen. I let their lack of confidence hamper me. When they told me I couldn't handle the work, I began to assume they were right."

Insecure and inexperienced, Janey realized that if she were ever going to survive as a ranger, she'd have to take matters into her own hands. As a starting point she chose the huge red fire truck the park kept to put out fires that might occur in the buildings.

Early one morning, when no one else was in the firehouse where the truck was parked, Janey entered the building and climbed onto the driver's seat. The dashboard in front of her was filled with dials, levers, buttons, and gauges. It looked like the cockpit of a jet plane. After she'd stared at the controls for a while, she slipped down from the seat and inched along the side of the truck. Touching the levers that operated hoses, pumps, and ladders; looking inside compartments full of tools, wheel chocks, fire helmets, rubber boots and coats, Janey was apprehensive. Scared, in fact. The fire truck was the most complex piece of machinery she'd ever examined.

Nearby hundreds of feet of hose hung on a rack. Janey wondered why it wasn't on the truck. Later she learned that after fire hose has been used, it must be drained and thoroughly dried before it can be repacked. As she stood back to look at the imposing collection of fire-fighting apparatus,

Janey knew she could not even begin to study it without an operator's manual.

She borrowed a manual. During the next few days she read and reread instructions, going back to the firehouse often to compare the diagrams in the book with the controls. When she felt that she had a good idea of the way the truck worked, she asked her supervisor if she could take it for a trial run.

Since he had not yet decided what to do with her, the supervisor seemed relieved that Janey was finding ways to keep herself busy. And since the truck had to be driven every few days to make certain that the battery was operating, he agreed to let her drive it. But he stipulated that another ranger go along to keep an eye on things.

Driving the truck was a bigger job than she'd expected. Instead of four gears it had eight, with some halfway positions between gears. With the other ranger beside her, Janey gripped the steering wheel, white-knuckled, as she drove around the park. "It was tricky," she says. "All those gears! But I made it; I didn't hit anything." In the following weeks she went to every fire drill and learned to use the rest of the fire equipment.

Once she'd mastered the fire truck, Janey wanted to learn traffic-accident investigation. "It's hard to do those things all by yourself," she says. "You need a little backup, a little encouragement." Since help wasn't forthcoming, she went back to the manuals, reading all she could about investigating accidents. When traffic accidents occurred in the park, she went out to observe how other rangers handled them. On the day she wrote her first traffic ticket, she was a little slow, but she got it right.

Winter came, blanketing the high desert country with a layer of snow. Janey taught herself to cross-country ski, a useful skill in any park where hikers might be stranded in the snow. By this time she'd made a friend, who let her use his 38-caliber handgun. Janey practiced shooting on the target range. One evening a week she drove to Cortez, Colorado, to take a course that would certify her as an emergency medical technician. Even if she had to do it on her own, she was determined to learn the skills she would need in protection work. But there were times when her determination wavered. "Up to a certain point I felt that I could do it and I wanted to show that I could, but I was almost convinced at times that I was making a big mistake."

Summer arrived, bringing visitors who toured the Indian ruins of Mesa Verde. For six hundred years, from A.D. 600 to 1200, Mesa Verde Indians had lived on tabletop mesas in that southwest corner of Colorado. Then they abandoned the mesas to move their homes high into the cliffs, which must have been an enormous job. Yet they remained in the cliff dwellings for only another hundred years. For reasons that are still not understood but probably had to do with drought, the Indians disappeared from Mesa Verde after A.D. 1300, leaving behind more than eight hundred dwellings containing well-preserved artifacts: pot shards, baskets, animal snares, even the mummified body of a baby girl.

When white men discovered the area in 1888, they dug carelessly through the ruins, destroying many priceless artifacts and selling others. To protect this important record of American history, our government created the Mesa Verde National Park in 1906. Most of the Indian ruins are closed to the public because the passage of centuries has left them structurally delicate. Those the public may visit have been stabilized with extra concrete added here and there so that visitors who walk over them won't break them down. The main job of park rangers is to keep people away from the

LEFT: A ranger in the protection division, Janey handles traffic investigations.

BELOW: Now an expert marksman, Janey first learned to shoot with a borrowed .38 caliber handgun.

ruins that are closed, and Janey took it upon herself to help with this work. She still hadn't been given definite assignments.

The summer months also brought seasonal rangers to help in the park. They were mostly college students and teachers who had been lucky enough to be hired by the Park Service during school vacation. Although they were all men, the seasonals accepted Janey readily. Unlike the permanent rangers, they had no doubt that she could perform protection work. During those months, at least, Janey felt that she was part of a team, but at the end of the summer she was returned to her uncertain status.

She had been at Mesa Verde for eighteen months when, for the second time in three years, an act of Congress made a difference in Janey's life. The Department of Interior was instructed by Congress to provide four hundred hours of training to all park rangers involved in law enforcement. Since Janey was in the protection division, she was included in the directive. In March 1975, she went to Washington, D.C., for fourteen weeks of training at the Consolidated Law Enforcement Center, where all federal law-enforcement officers are trained.

At the center, Janey took classes in constitutional law, criminal law, court procedures, and report-writing. She learned interviewing techniques and traffic-accident investigation in addition to practical skills like self-defense and the use of handguns and long guns. All the things Janey had tried so hard to learn on her own were now taught to her by experienced instructors who believed that women were as capable as men. "I found out then that I could perform well," Janey states. "When I graduated fifth in a class of fifty, that helped my confidence a lot."

Returning to Mesa Verde in June, Janey discovered that the chief ranger had been transferred and replaced by a new chief, who was much more open-minded about a woman on his staff. With an unbiased boss and her newly learned skills in protection, Janey was no longer the stepchild in the park family. And when she was invited to give law-enforcement training to that summer's staff of seasonal workers, she knew she was an accepted, respected professional, the kind of park ranger she had always wanted to be.

## LAW ENFORCEMENT

*O*nly two weeks after Janey's return to Mesa Verde, an event occurred in South Dakota that would bring her to the summit of the four stone heads on Mount Rushmore.

The Pine Ridge Indian Reservation in South Dakota is 50 miles deep and 100 miles wide, home to fifteen thousand people. Ten thousand of them belong to the tribe of Oglala Sioux, among the poorest of all native Americans. Murders, beatings, and violent disagreements had plagued the reservation, where members of a militant group, the American Indian Movement, were at odds with the more conservative tribal government.

Under the hot noonday sun of June 26, two FBI agents drove toward a cluster of rundown farmhouses where several American Indian Movement supporters were known to be staying. The FBI agents carried warrants for the arrest of four Indians who were wanted on a kidnapping charge. As the agents got out of their cars, they were struck by rifle fire.

They fell to the ground, but managed to reach a car radio to call for help.

Within minutes, ten other officers reached the scene, and the number of police cars speeding down the dirt road increased rapidly as word of the ambush spread. No one knew how many Indians were in the main farmhouse. Rifles cracked in sporadic cross fire between the two groups as the shoot-out continued for six hours through the heat and dust of the afternoon. When officers lobbed tear-gas cannisters into the farmhouse, the Indians inside escaped through the back door. They disappeared into grass-covered bottomland and along a wooded creek bank behind the houses.

Three men's bodies were found that evening, two of them the FBI agents who had gone to serve the warrant, the third an eighteen-year-old Indian youth.

With darkness, an uneasy quiet fell over the reservation, but during the early morning hours of June 27, a blast ripped the visitors' center at Mount Rushmore National Memorial, 35 miles from Pine Ridge. No one was hurt. The explosives had gone off at 4 A.M. on the viewing terrace. Two glass walls in a building that faced the four stone heads had shattered, dashing glass fragments over the terrace and the building.

That day a call went out to supervisors of all national parks in the Rocky Mountain region, asking for rangers trained in law enforcement to patrol Mount Rushmore. Three years earlier a group of Indians who believed that the Rushmore area rightfully belonged to native Americans had taken over the mountain for a short time. They established an encampment just behind the giant heads. The bombing of the visitors' center might signal another attempted takeover, or it might be connected to the shoot-out at Pine Ridge. No one was certain. With the Fourth of July weekend coming, thousands of visitors would arrive at the memorial to view the four carved faces. The Park Service staff was responsible for the safety of those visitors.

Janey was called to the superintendent's office, where he explained the situation to her. "I'd like to send you as one of the two volunteers from Mesa Verde, if you're willing," he told her.

"That would be great," she replied.

Flying to Mount Rushmore, Janey was tense and excited about her first law-enforcement assignment. When she reached the memorial she met the other members of the team. They were sharp-looking professionals, the kind of people she'd feel privileged to work with. Janey was the only woman in the group.

The twenty-four outside rangers reinforced the Mount Rushmore ranger staff and the park police. They were divided into a day shift and a night shift, each team to work twelve-hour stretches of duty. Janey drew the day shift. Every morning brought a different duty—patrolling the visitors' paths in the parklike area, riding patrol cars on the roads to watch for possible demonstrators. More strenuous was the foot patrol on the sides of the mountain leading to the four stone faces. For twelve hours Janey and a partner would hike through brush and trees to scan the area, making sure that no one was trying to scale the elevation. There were no foot paths because visitors were not allowed on the mountain.

Most dramatic was duty atop 6,200-foot Mount Rushmore. Janey and four or five other rangers made the thirty-minute climb, carrying food to last them through the twelve-hour shift. From the top they had a wide view of the visitors' center below and the surrounding Black Hills, dark with thick stands of conifers. Janey and the others tried to stay just behind the heads so that visitors looking up at the carved faces through binoculars would not be aware that the mountain was being heavily guarded against any possible threat to the memorial.

When American artist Gutzon Borglum sculpted the mountain during the years between 1927 and 1941, he began to build a vault behind the stone heads. Janey took time to explore the open enclosure. According to Borglum's plans, the vault would hold sealed copies of the Declaration of Independence and the Constitution. The walls of the granite vault were to be inscribed with a brief history of the United States in three languages. Carved in granite deep inside the mountain, the inscriptions would be safe from erosion so that thousands of years from now, people would understand Mount Rushmore's historical significance. But the Hall of Records, as Borglum named it, was never completed.

Gutzon Borglum was enthralled with his sculptures. In his own words, he tried to "find and release the faces of four great Americans within that granite mountain." He eagerly reported, "The brow [of Washington] has emerged, amazing in mass, vigor, and beauty of form . . . the great face seemed to belong to the mountain. It took on the elemental courage of the rocks surrounding it."

In spite of Borglum's visionary bent of mind, he did an incredible engineering job in sculpting the rock with dynamite. Washington, Jefferson, Theodore Roosevelt, and Lincoln stare solemnly from the granite, white under bright sunshine, buff-colored at twilight. Two million visitors come each year to marvel at the colossal proportions of four presidential faces.

During that holiday week of 1975, the visitors may have noticed an unusually large number of uniformed rangers and park police patrolling the area, but few bothered to ask questions, which was the way the rangers wanted it. As things turned out, no disturbance marred the holidays, perhaps because of the heavy security.

On emergency call twenty-four hours each day, Janey answers a radio message.

Though the hours were long, Janey enjoyed being part of the law-enforcement detail. "I was accepted as a member of the team. Nobody said, 'Oh, she can't do it because she's female.' I just did everything everyone else did." At the end of two weeks Janey said good-bye to the other members of the team, not knowing that they would be brought together again.

The Bicentennial was approaching, a possible target date for militant demonstrators. In February 1976, Park Service administrators decided to make the team of twenty-four law-enforcement rangers official; they called it the Special Activities Group. The SAG members would continue to work at their regularly assigned parks, but if trouble threatened, they could be flown quickly to the problem area. To prepare for this work, Janey and the other SAG rangers went to Denver, Colorado, for a week's training on the rifle range and in the gym, where they were taught to disarm people. FBI instructors gave lectures on terrorist groups and the way they operated. The Special Activities Group spent hours learning the properties of explosive devices they might have to deal with.

Mount Rushmore would be the center for a big Bicentennial celebration on July 4, 1976. Once more, to guard against any possible flare-up of trouble, Janey went with the SAG rangers to the memorial, but once again, all was quiet. She worked nights that time, from 8 P.M. to 8 A.M.

At eight o'clock on the morning of July 4, Janey left Mount Rushmore and drove to the motel where she was staying. After twelve hours of patrolling foot trails in the dark, all she wanted was to get into bed. But when she arrived at the motel, she found a message. She was to call the chief ranger at Yellowstone National Park.

Yawning, wondering what it was all about, Janey placed the call.

"Mary Jane McDowell?" a man's voice said. "We have an opening for a ranger here at Yellowstone. Would you be interested in filling the position?"

She didn't even have to think about it before she said yes. "To a ranger, Yellowstone is like Mecca," Janey declares, "or at least it was to me. It's the most famous and the largest of all the national parks, with all that wildlife and those thermal pools. After I accepted and hung up the phone, I wasn't the least bit sleepy anymore. What a way to celebrate the Fourth!"

## YELLOWSTONE

*A*s far back as the early 1800s, rumors reached Americans of a region where water spouted in great columns, where a cliff of black glass glittered in the sunlight, where mud bubbled from the core of the earth. Though the rumors had spread from the reports of explorers John Colter and James Bridger, most people thought such fantastic yarns couldn't be true. In 1870, a party headed by surveyor Henry Washburn and Army officer Gustavus Doane led an official expedition to explore Yellowstone country. They found that the territory was even more incredible than anyone could have imagined.

Seated around a campfire one night near the end of their month-long scouting trip, the men talked about what should be done with the area. By law, they could have filed claims on the land to log the thick stands of timber, or to hunt and trap and mine. Or they could have claimed it and charged people a fee to see the spectacular wonders. One man in the party, a territorial judge named Cornelius Hedges, suggested that such extraordinary land should not belong to individuals but to all the American people. The others came to agree with his opinion.

On March 1, 1872, President Ulysses S. Grant signed a bill creating Yellowstone National Park "as a public park or pleasuring ground for the benefit and enjoyment of the people," the first national park in the world.

By the 1970s, the people were enjoying it so much that Janey had to start doing her ranger work the moment she arrived. Her new position was as subdistrict ranger; she would supervise eight other rangers (male) assigned to the area.

Janey arrived at Yellowstone in August, at the height of the tourist season. It seemed to her that all of the two million plus annual visitors must have been in the park that day. Campgrounds were filled to capacity with trailers, motor homes, tents of every size and shape, and sleeping bags spread over what remained of the ground. Cars crept bumper-to-bumper on the loop of road leading to and from Old Faithful. Yellowstone National Park was overwhelmed with its own success.

Yet most of the visitors were crowded into a very small portion of the park, the five percent with paved roads, parking lots, and visitors' centers. Only a few hardy backpackers ventured into the untouched backcountry. They saw it as it had been a hundred years earlier, when Yellowstone's future was decided.

On her first day, while one of the rangers took Janey riding in a Park Service car to show her the area, a call came on the car radio. A little girl had wandered away from her family in the picnic grounds, and was lost. Would they please find her?

As they drove toward the picnic grounds, Janey wondered how she could possibly find a lost child when she couldn't even find her own way around the district. But the ranger who was with her drove slowly along the road through the trees, calling the little girl's name again and again over the car's loudspeaker. It worked. The child walked out of the woods to the car. The parents were tearfully grateful, and Janey was relieved.

After Labor Day, when schools opened everywhere, Yellowstone was almost deserted. Families with children had driven out of the park as suddenly as the birds soared into the sky to fly south.

"It was like magic," Janey remembers. "At that point traffic really dropped off. It was as though I had the whole park to myself."

That autumn Janey became acquainted with the immensity of Yellowstone. In October, when cottonwood leaves spun gold along the creekbeds, she rode horseback into the backcountry for a two-week pack trip with her future supervisor, Jerry Mernin. They led a packhorse loaded with provisions to stock ranger cabins. During hunting season rangers patrol the park to make certain that no one is hunting illegally inside park boundaries. Jerry and Janey would do that while they were stocking the cabins. Since the backcountry is so extensive, the log cabins where the rangers spent their nights had to be well supplied with food and fuel.

Before they started, Janey had her first lesson in loading a packhorse. "There's a real art to packing horses," she explains. "Although a packhorse can carry more than two hundred pounds, the load must be balanced exactly or the horse will get rubbed raw or will tire easily. And you have

Returning lost children is one of the more rewarding duties of a park ranger.

to tie all different kinds of knots for different loads. It's almost a lost art. Not too many people know how to do it anymore."

Janey and Jerry left the South Entrance on a cool but sunny day, fording the Snake River and then traveling through the forest of lodgepole pines. Lodgepoles are tall, slender trees with little greenery on the lower part of their trunks. They cover 80 percent of Yellowstone, and got their name because Indians found them ideal for holding up tepees. Stands of lodgepole are so thick that if a tree dies, it may never fall to the ground. It is caught in the branches of the trees surrounding it to lean at an odd angle for years.

In the lodgepole forest in the autumn, bull elk rip the silence with their eerie buglelike bellowing. Grizzlies lumber along a clearing, or stand with their broad necks stretched to sniff the air. Woodpeckers rattle the tops of trees while flocks of Canada geese fly their arrowhead formations high overhead. The beauty of the Yellowstone autumn filled all of Janey's senses.

By evening they had reached the first cabin on their route. Like other cabins in Yellowstone, this one had a descriptive name—Harebell. After they unloaded the packhorse, Jerry showed Janey how to picket the animals: One end of a rope is tied around a foreleg and the other fastened to a stake in the ground, allowing the horse to walk in a circle to graze. Unless it was picketed, the horse would trot off toward home during the night.

Once the animals had been cared for, Janey had a chance to look inside the cabin. The first thing she noticed was bedding hanging from the ceiling.

"What are those blankets doing up there?" she asked.

"They're up there because if they were left stacked on the beds, mice would nest in them," Jerry told her. "We have enough trouble with mice without having to shake them out of our blankets."

As they unpacked the food, Janey could see that the whole cabin had been mouse-proofed. All the food except the canned goods and the perishables was stored inside a tight metal cabinet. Beneath a trapdoor in the floor, food that could spoil was kept in a root cellar where the temperature never dropped below freezing. Fresh eggs would last for months.

After the food was put away and a fire crackled in the wood-burning stove, Janey noticed that the walls of the cabin were covered with names, penciled or carved, of rangers. "Stocking cabins, Oct. 28, 1940," she read, and "Winter ski trip, March 3 & 4, 1934," with a list of names beneath. "It was like reading the whole history of the park."

Having ridden for so many hours through the fresh, chilly air, Janey was famished. Jerry showed her how to cook on a wood stove; it was tricky, because the heat varied with the amount of wood stacked inside. After they'd eaten by the light of gas lanterns, Janey found herself growing drowsy from the warmth of the stove, so she took the blankets down from the rafters to make up her bed.

"That was only a four-blanket night," she remembers. "In the middle of winter, when the temperature goes way down below zero, you need six of those Army blankets. They're itchy, and they're so heavy that when you're underneath six of them, it's hard to turn over, especially since the mattresses sag in the middle. You have to literally pull yourself out of bed in the morning."

From the time women first began to apply for nontraditional jobs, one of the arguments used against them was that women and men would have to work together on field trips, and would have to share the same facilities and the same sleeping quarters. How could modesty be observed, the opponents argued, when women and men were in such close proximity?

Just as beauty is in the eye of the beholder, modesty is in the mind of the practitioner. Most of the ranger cabins have only one room, but privacy is easy to maintain. When the gas lantern went out, its bright flame diminishing little by little until the cabin was in total darkness, Janey was under the blankets, changing into her pajamas and draping her clothes over a chair next to the bed. Since the fire in the wood stove had burned down, it was too cold to undress anywhere except under the covers anyway. And when she awakened at five-thirty in the morning, the cabin was really frigid. She shivered back into her clothes before getting out of bed, then hurried outside with Jerry to care for horses.

The half-mile hike to the spot where the horses had been picketed seemed spectral. Hardly a glimmer of dawn lightened the sky. In the morning chill they could feel the vapor from their breaths but couldn't see it.

Janey pried up the picket stake and untied the rope from her horse Eli, then climbed on him to ride bareback to the cabin. She'd never ridden bareback before, and she was holding the picket ropes in one hand. The forest was still dark as Eli crashed through the trees, hungry and anxious to get back to the cabin, where he knew he'd be fed. Suddenly Janey glimpsed the shape of a large fallen log directly in their path. Certain she would be thrown, she gripped with her knees, gritted her teeth, and clutched the halter rope as Eli soared over the log like a steeplechase racer. By some miracle, she stayed on.

Back at the cabin, Janey grained the horses. Animals are always fed first in the wilderness, people later. After breakfast and several cups of coffee to warm them against the chill, the two rangers mounted and rode out to patrol the boundaries in the southeast corner of the park. No hunting is allowed in Yellowstone, but hunters do occasionally stray inside park borders. Usually it's by mistake, which is very different from the old days, when the park was being devastated by trespassers.

Although Yellowstone was declared a protected area in 1872, it was protected in name only. No money was appropriated by Congress for a park staff. Even though hostile Indians were still a threat, white game poachers and trophy hunters trespassed to shoot buffalo, elk, bighorn sheep, and anything else that moved. Lumbermen cut trees and hauled away logs by the wagonload. Miners searched for gold, while trappers did a thriving business in furs. The pillage became so wanton that the Secretary of the Interior (national parks are administered by the Interior Department) asked the Secretary of the Army for help. In 1886, a division of the United States Cavalry arrived to patrol Yellowstone.

But the park was vast, and illegal hunters took their chances on evading the soldiers. By the end of the nineteenth century, the 60 million bison that had once roamed the West had been slaughtered almost to extinction. Their rarity made them even more valuable to trophy hunters, who wanted massive buffalo heads mounted on walls of their homes. In 1894, a single poacher killed eighty buffalo in Yellowstone before he was caught by a Cavalry trooper. That was estimated to be one fourth of the total number of bison then surviving in the United States.

Though Janey and Jerry saw several hunting parties in the hours when they patrolled the boundaries, none of the hunters were inside the park. Instead they waited at the borders, knowing that elk migrate out of the park in October. Today's hunting regulations prevent anything like the thoughtless slaughter of the past century.

It was time to move onto other cabins that needed restocking, but before they left Harebell, Janey and Jerry had to replenish the wood supply. Throughout the summer, other park employees had scouted for dead trees in the area, cutting the fallen trunks with hand saws and leaving sections of log known as rounds. Janey went to work with an axe, splitting the rounds into stovewood.

When Harebell was stocked, cleaned, sealed against animals, and locked against trespassers, Janey and Jerry started for the other cabins that needed supplies—Howell, Thoroughfare, and Fox Creek. Yellowstone is full of descriptive names. By the end of two weeks, when they returned to the South Entrance, riding through a thick whiteness of snow untouched except for the horses' prints, Janey was calling the park "home."

## YELLOWSTONE NATIONAL PARK IN WINTER

*I*n winter, Yellowstone is cold, still, snow-bound, and incredibly beautiful. Janey spent her first Yellowstone winter in a small apartment at Grant Village, on the southwestern shore of Yellowstone Lake. Two road-maintenance men and their wives lived in adjoining apartments, but Janey was the only ranger there.

"It was like living in a basement," she says. "The snow was six feet deep, reaching almost to the tops of my windows. The first thing I did each morning was to go out and measure the snow depth, climbing up a flight of steps which had been carved out of snow from my back door to a packed path around the apartment. If I stepped off the packed snow, I'd sink way down into white powder."

Though all of Yellowstone's roads are closed to cars and trucks during the winter months, a few hundred snowmobilers arrive at the park each day for winter recreation. They travel along highways on which the snow has been packed densely by large snow-grooming machines. Stakes are planted along the roads at 30-foot intervals, because when the white drifts blow hard, only the stakes let travelers know whether they're still on the roads. It was Janey's job to patrol the highways and assist visitors whose snowmobiles might have broken down or become stuck in the drifts.

On those frigid winter days she wore long underwear,

wool pants, her ranger uniform with a wool sweater or vest, and a bulky long-zippered snowmobile suit. Her face was protected by a silk mask worn beneath a yellow visored helmet. Several pairs of socks under heavy boots kept her feet from freezing, but her hands were vulnerable to the cold because they stayed, unmoving, on the handlebars. The snowmobile's speed of 40 miles per hour created a wind-chill factor, which worsened the 10-degree average winter temperature. To keep her hands functioning, Janey wore two pairs of gloves inside Army surplus mitts designed for Arctic expeditions. The mitts reached her elbows. "Wearing that

As October snow blankets Yellowstone, Janey leads a pack horse on the way to stock ranger cabins.

many clothes, I lumbered along like a bear. I couldn't have run if I had to."

One morning Janey started out to Mammoth Hot Springs, a 60-mile trip from Grant Village. Because the brakes had gone out on her snowmobile, she had to drive it to Mammoth for repairs. Behind the snowmobile she pulled a sled loaded with cargo consisting of the two packs she always hauled while she was on patrol. One was filled with food, a hot drink in a thermos, a container of oxygen, first-aid supplies, matches, extra socks, gloves, and wool caps. The other kit held a radio, tools, and fan belts to make minor repairs on stranded snowmobiles.

The underground thermal activity of Yellowstone creates "hot spots," which stay warm all year long, melting snow and ice around Old Faithful and Hayden Valley and allowing grass to remain fresh and green. Moose, elk, and buffalo graze on the fresh grass in the winter, then wander along the snowpacked highways to avoid floundering in the softer snow. The road to Mammoth Hot Springs, the road Janey traveled that day, runs directly through Hayden Valley.

She took her eyes off the road for a moment as she looked behind her to make certain that the cargo hadn't shifted in her snowmobile sled. When she glanced back at the road again, she was horrified to see a buffalo standing only 4 feet ahead of her on a direct collision course. Screaming inside her helmet, Janey dragged her feet on the snow to slow her speed as she swerved the snowmobile to miss the buffalo— by inches. "If we had collided, it would have been good-bye Janey," she declared. "Those animals weigh half a ton, literally, and I didn't have any brakes."

Two days later, on her way back from Mammoth Hot Springs, Janey again came upon buffalo on the road, three of them, a bull, a cow, and a calf. This time she had brakes, and she wasn't about to blunder into another confrontation with the huge beasts. "We have a saying in the park," Janey mentions. "You can make a buffalo go anywhere it wants to go." She waited in the snow for an hour and a half before the buffalo family finally meandered far enough to the side of the road to let her whiz past.

Snowmobilers aren't the only park visitors who have problems in the winter. Cross-country skiers come to Yellowstone, too, to travel the trails leading to Old Faithful and other geysers. If a column of water and steam is awesome during the summer season, it's even more spectacular as it erupts through a blanket of ice and snow into air so cold that the steam expands into billowing clouds. Near Janey's living quarters, steam from the geyser basins would condense on the trees, where it froze in layer on layer until the evergreens were coated ethereally with thick clumps of white ice. Janey called them "ghost trees."

The skiers would usually stay for a few days inside the park, spending the nights in lightweight, but warm, sleeping bags inside tents they carried in backpacks. Sometimes novice skiers discovered that they weren't adequately equipped for such cold weather. If they became too chilled to go on, Janey would meet them at a trail head and deliver them, on her snowmobile, to an entrance station.

On Christmas Eve during that first winter, Janey had an early dinner with ranger friends at Old Faithful, then returned to her apartment. Because she planned to spend Christmas day with Jerry, his wife, and a number of other winter rangers in Jerry's home at the South Entrance station, she worked late into the evening, fixing salads and desserts to take to the party. Carols from the stereo filled her tiny kitchen as she arranged her handiwork like a tableau on the table top. The final hour of Christmas Eve was drawing to a close, and Janey decided that she wanted to be outside.

After dressing warmly, she took her skis and climbed the snow steps from her back door to ground level. "The full moon was so bright that it made tree-shadows on the snow," she remembers. "As I skied across the valley I could see stars, even though they were dimmed by the brilliant light from the moon. Far off in the stillness, I heard a coyote serenade the night. It was just past midnight, the first minute of the most beautiful Christmas I ever spent."

Later that winter Janey skied into the Heart Lake district with Jerry and another ranger named John to check the ski trails and to shovel snow from the backcountry cabin roofs. They stayed the night in one of the cabins, where Janey baked ham, sweet potatoes, and homemade biscuits in the wood stove. "That was a seven-blanket night," Janey says. "We got up at four A.M. to get an early start, because it takes forever to get everything ready when it's so cold. After we built the fire and ate breakfast, we waxed our skis while we waited for it to get light outside. John went out to check the temperature so that we'd know how to wax our skis. You use different kinds of wax for different degrees of cold. When he came back inside, he didn't say a word, so I went to look at the thermometer. It was thirty below zero."

By eight in the morning they were skiing across frozen Heart Lake, examining each other's faces often to make certain that their small amounts of exposed skin weren't becoming frostbitten. "It was so cold that I could actually see the air," Janey recalls. "It was a pinkish-blue color that was really amazing. I felt almost as though I could reach out and the air would break over me. It was so still, no air movement at all, just like suspended ice crystals. And I could hear the ice in Heart Lake cracking and groaning and creaking."

They skied 17 miles that day. By sunset they had reached

the Snake River, where they climbed into a tublike cart suspended from a steel cable that stretches from bank to bank above the river. Since the cable dips in the middle of the span, gravity propelled their cart to the low center halfway across. Then the rangers used a steel handle to pull the cart along the cable to the other side. Fortunately Jerry's house was only a short distance from the river bank. Once inside, Janey warmed herself with a hot toddy before heading for an even hotter bubble bath. "I spent a lot of time in bathtubs full of hot water that winter," Janey says, "because after four or six or eight hours in subfreezing weather, that was the only way I could get my body temperature back to normal."

Many people ask Janey how rangers manage to keep themselves busy at Yellowstone in the winter, when there are so few visitors. "It's true that in the winter we don't have so many duties," she explains, "but it takes so much longer to do each thing that every duty becomes a major undertaking. The hours of daylight are short because we're so far north; the sun rises at eight A.M. and sets at four P.M. Getting into all the necessary clothing takes a lot of time. If I've been out patrolling for four or five hours, which is as long as I can normally stand the cold, that gets me back home at about three in the afternoon. Then I get gas for the snowmobile. I have to mix my own gas and oil, which takes a while because the oil gets thick from the cold. I pull the snowmobile into the garage to clean it and check it and regas it. That takes an hour. Then I go inside and hang up all my snowmobile clothes to dry. After that I take a hot bath to warm myself, and fuss a lot over making supper. The evenings are long and I seldom see anyone, but I'm never lonely. Even though I can get one television station in the park, I rarely watch TV. I read a lot. All in all, it's as nice a way to spend the winter as any I know."

# BEARS

*S*ix species of large grazing animals live in Yellowstone: deer, elk, buffalo, bighorn sheep, antelope, and moose. Under natural conditions, the populations of these herds rise and fall, depending on the amount of food available to them. Park officials tried in years past to preserve the herds during harsh winters by giving them extra feed, but this turned out to be a self-defeating practice. When the animals were fed artificially, their numbers grew to such a point that they couldn't survive without help. It became clear that nature's way of preserving the herd size was best. If left undisturbed, nature weaves the lives of wild creatures into a well-balanced tapestry, which lets the herds increase in years of abundance and decrease in lean years. Just as human interference with the grazing herds, though well-intentioned, was misguided, people's meddling with the bears in Yellowstone proved to be a very serious mistake.

When the big bears emerge from their dens in the spring, hungry after a long winter's rest, they feast on carcasses of the elk, moose, and buffalo that did not live through the winter. By midsummer they range through the backcountry, eating roots, leaves, berries, insects, and small rodents. This is the kind of natural diet that keeps bears in the best condition. But for a long period of time that ended only in recent years, Yellowstone bears regularly gorged themselves on handouts of junk food and garbage.

According to Janey, most visitors to Yellowstone have two top priority items on the list of sights they want to see: Old Faithful, and bears. Perhaps because bears stand upright and look like shaggy human giants, perhaps because their awesome strength excites bear-watchers with the possibility of sudden danger, people have always been fascinated by them. Indians called them "beasts that walk like men." Toddlers hug teddy bears in their beds at night and grow up feeling affection for Smokey Bear, Gentle Ben, and Yogi Bear.

Since people have always come to Yellowstone to see bears, during the 1950s and '60s park rangers did little to keep the bears away from park roads. Not only did the big animals forage, with the Park Service's blessing, in the 2,000 tons of garbage left behind by summer visitors, but they also stood along the edges of highways to beg for food like over-sized puppies. Janey says, "The rangers called them 'cookie bears.' They were eating marshmallows and cookies and candy. They weren't having to forage for themselves and find their own food, and they were bringing up their cubs to live on handouts, too." Even though it was illegal for visitors to feed bears, in those years the regulations against feeding were not strictly enforced.

If the visitors had been content to stay in their cars and just watch, the only result might have been the bears' loss of dignity and optimum health. But tourists wanted to take close-up pictures for the folks back home, or they wanted to reach out and pet the bears. The result was hundreds of bites, scratches, and clawings, which gave Yellowstone's bears an undeserved bad reputation.

In the early 1970s, park administrators closed the garbage dumps and became strict with visitors who fed bears. Once the artificial food supply was cut off, the bears began to drift again into the backcountry where they ate the sort of food nature intended them to eat. A few continued to insist on a visitor-supplied smorgasbord of people's food, and these bears were tranquilized with dart guns, loaded into cages, and flown by helicopter into the backcountry. In her first full summer at the park, Janey went along on one of those bear-trapping expeditions.

A sow grizzly bear with her two cubs had been sighted wandering through Fishing Bridge campground, just east of where the Yellowstone River flows out of Yellowstone Lake. A single bear-sighting is not a cause for alarm because a bear may just be passing through on its way to the back-country, but after a second sighting of the same bear, the rangers begin a careful watch. The third time that particular bear and her cubs had visited Fishing Bridge campground, the rangers knew she was not going to go away of her own volition. She would have to be removed bodily to prevent any danger to the campers.

After dark, because bears roam mostly at night, Janey rode in a Park Service van with the district ranger to a loop of road circling the campground. Other rangers waited in patrol cars at adjoining loops. Two hours passed quietly before Janey and Roger, the district ranger, heard a terse announcement on the van's radio. "She's here!"

With the van lights out, they drove slowly to the next loop of road and sure enough, there was a mother grizzly with her cubs. The bear wasn't rummaging in garbage cans because the cans are sealed tightly to keep bears out; she was ambling around the grounds with her two cubs at her heels.

When bears are to be tranquilized with dart guns, the amount of tranquilizer has to be measured precisely, based on the bears' weight, so that they won't be harmed. Roger watched the shadowy forms of the moving animals and was able to estimate their weights. He put Janey in charge of filling the darts with tranquilizer, telling her the exact amounts to use. By flashlight, Janey inserted a syringe into

# ENJOY THEM AT A DISTANCE

## PARK BEARS AND OTHER ANIMALS ARE DANGEROUS

Don't encourage them to approach.

Park regulations prohibit feeding or molesting animals.

Stop cars in pullouts ONLY — not on roadway.

Keep car windows closed when near bears.

**THIS WARNING IS FOR YOUR PROTECTION**

# ABOUT BEARS

Like all animals in our National Parks, bears are wild animals. Because of their protected status they have lost their fear of man. While this may make them appear tame, actually in this state they are more dangerous.

Troublesome bears are trapped and removed to remote areas of the park, or in extreme cases must be destroyed. In order that visitors may continue to enjoy the sight of bears roaming freely in our National Parks, and to avoid personal injury, please follow these suggestions when camping:

Keep a clean camp and use a minimum of odorous food. Seal surplus food in clean wrapping material or in airtight containers. Ice chests are generally not bear proof. A good deodorizer is effective in eliminating food odors from your camp.

Food left on tables or stored in a tent in open boxes or food containers is a natural target for bears and an invitation for bear damage. Back country campers often suspend their supplies between two trees out of bear's reach.

Food should not be stored in vehicles with convertible tops. Properly wrapped or sealed food is normally safe when stored in the trunk of a hard-topped car provided all windows are closed.

Burn all garbage and food containers. Do not bury food scraps and containers. In the back country pack out any noncombustible litter to the nearest trash containers provided.

**REPORT ANY BEAR DAMAGE OR PERSONAL INJURIES TO A PARK RANGER IMMEDIATELY.**

 **U.S. DEPARTMENT OF THE INTERIOR**

**NATIONAL PARK SERVICE**  ☆G.P.O. —622-294 3-1

the end of a bottle of liquid tranquilizer, just as a doctor does when he's going to give a shot. Then she squirted the fluid into the darts, which are metal tubes with long needles on one end and feathers on the other.

Janey handed the first dart to Roger. He would have to hit the mother grizzly first; if he hit one of the cubs, the sow would react with savage maternal fury. Roger slipped the dart into the gun, aimed the barrel carefully through the van window, and fired.

The "whoosh" of the shot shredded the stillness as the dart struck the mother grizzly's shoulder. Janey knew that the she-bear had been hit because the animal gave a deep grunt. Within minutes, the big animal dropped to the ground, unable to move but still conscious.

Janey and Roger had to rush to tranquilize the cubs, since the drug's action is short-lived. As soon as the mother could function again, she would try to defend her babies. When all three bears were helpless and the vehicles' headlights had been turned on so the rangers could see, Janey, Roger, and five other rangers ran to drag in the 300-pound sow. They hauled her to a cage built from culvert pipe, then dropped a gridlike gate over the open end. They carried the cubs to another cage.

The rangers then left to wait for daylight. By morning, when they returned to the animals once again, the three grizzlies were wide-awake and howling mad. Even though the traps were tightly closed, Janey stayed well out of the range of those protruding grizzly claws. When the animals were sedated Roger opened the cages with great caution. Yellowstone rangers like to trade stories about bears that were thought to be safely asleep but turned out to be awake and bent on vengeance.

The three grizzlies were lifted out of their traps and placed in a single large net, which was flown by helicopter to the backcountry. When the net was landed, a research biologist opened it, gave all three bears an antidote to the sedative, and ran like mad back to the helicopter before the mother grizzly could recover from her grogginess. Three more grizzlies had been returned to the wild, where they could roam freely and where they would no longer be a threat to visitors in the park campgrounds.

Bears are like rattlesnakes: When they meet people, they'd just as soon turn around and go the other way. A park superintendent has said, "If bears *enjoyed* conflict, we'd lose a lot more people."

Though bears don't go out of their way to pick fights with people, mother bears with cubs are unpredictable and dangerous. On June 13, 1978, a twenty-one-year-old woman named Marianna Young arrived at Yellowstone to hike the trail to Heart Lake. Because she'd been working as a summer waitress in adjoining Grand Teton National Park, Marianna wanted to get away from people for a while to be by herself. When she parked her car at the trail head, she saw a lot of cars and trucks already parked there, with a large group of people preparing to hike the same trail. There were twenty-seven hikers in the party, all from Texas. Marianna hurried as she put on her hiking boots so that she could start out ahead of them.

The trail to Heart Lake is 8 miles long; Marianna had walked the first mile when she came to a little rise where the trail narrowed. Because some lodgepole pines had fallen close to the trail, Marianna walked with her eyes lowered to look out for obstacles. When she glanced up, she saw a mother grizzly and three small cubs on the other side of the rise, walking 100 feet ahead of her in the same direction.

Animal behaviorists believe that a mother bear with cubs insists on a certain amount of space when she travels, as though she draws an invisible perimeter around her. If anyone comes through that perimeter, the grizzly considers her space violated and attacks, but Marianna was not aware of this.

"I stopped and took off my pack," Marianna recalls, "to get out my camera. The mother grizzly started to sniff as if she smelled me. She turned around and sniffed and then she turned back, kind of like she wasn't sure where I was, but she knew that someone was there. When she spotted me she started toward me, making a really loud noise like a roar. She was coming at me like a ten-ton train. I think I tried to climb a tree and then I started to run. I'm sure it didn't take long at all for her to get to me. She picked me up once and threw me. She literally picked me up off the ground and just threw me like I was a sack of garbage."

Marianna tried to play dead. It's generally agreed that if a bear victim can lie perfectly still, the bear will probably quit attacking and go away. But in her terror, Marianna couldn't stop screaming as the bear clawed and bit her chest, thighs, and back. She says, "I don't think I ever tried to fight her, but I was yelling and screaming a whole lot, until I couldn't yell anymore. After I'd gotten to the point where I wasn't making any noise or moving any longer, she must have thought I was dead, so she left. As she was leaving, she tore off part of my scalp. I don't know whether she used her teeth or her claws, but I think it was her claws."

Marianna lay torn and bleeding 15 feet from the trail, her blonde hair matted with blood, several ribs smashed and massive wounds gaping. Within five minutes the first members of the hiking group from Texas came along the trail toward her. "I could hear the people coming," Marianna says. "I could hear them talking before they got to me. I yelled something and I saw them walking toward me, but I couldn't see them clearly."

Two men from the group hurried back to the trail head to

drive for help. Others did what they could for Marianna, wetting her bandanna and pressing it to her lips, covering her with a blanket to keep the flies away. At the suggestion of one of the hikers, most of the group stood at the side of the trail yelling and singing to frighten off the bear, although by that time the sow and cubs were probably a good distance away.

"I really didn't think I was going to make it," Marianna remembers, "because I kept having trouble breathing. The people who helped me were praying, and they talked to me, and they went through my pack to look for identification to see who I was. The bear must have gone through my pack, too, after she attacked me, because it was ripped to shreds. She'd taken all my dried apricots and the rest of the food I'd brought. I guess the cubs helped her eat it."

The two hikers who'd gone for help sped south until they saw a marked patrol car parked along the side of the road. Inside the car was Gary, one of the seasonal rangers who was working for Janey that summer. When the men told Gary that a girl had been hurt by a bear on the Heart Lake trail, he radioed Janey at Grant Village. The call was also picked up by other rangers at South Entrance. Since Gary was the ranger closest to the victim, Janey instructed him to speed to the accident scene with first-aid supplies.

Janey and two seasonal rangers left Grant Village immediately with a Stokes litter (a type of stretcher) and all the first-aid supplies they could carry. With their siren wailing, they drove the 5 miles to the Heart Lake trail head, where they met rangers from South Entrance who had responded to the call for help. Janey left one of her rangers at the trail head, both to relay radio calls on the car radio (she and the others would have only radio handsets, which are not as powerful) and to keep other hikers from coming into the area.

Half a dozen of the hikers who had found Marianna were waiting at the trail head; Janey asked them to come with her to help carry out the victim. With the Stokes litter and the first-aid supplies, the rangers ran the mile to where Marianna lay. Gary had already administered first aid. "He did such a good job," Janey says. "Without knowing what he was going to find, because he didn't have any specific information about her condition, he had just guessed what to take in, and he had carried it all by himself. He took in these big Army-surplus battle dressings, which were what Marianna really needed because she had a lot of massive injuries to her stomach and her back. Gary had already applied these big dressings all the way around her and a dressing to the top of her head."

By the time Janey had checked Gary's work, her supervisor, Jerry, arrived. "Jerry was in charge from then on, and he told me to take over the first-aid responsibility."

Janey arranged blankets in the Stokes litter, and with the help of the others lifted Marianna from the ground onto the litter. Janey gave her oxygen. "She was going into shock fast, and there was so much to do, with stopping her bleeding and giving her oxygen. And also by that time, we were deciding whether it was faster to carry her out to the trail head and take her to the hospital or . . . to get a helicopter into the air."

They decided on the helicopter, radioing the park hospital to request that one be sent. Since a helicopter couldn't land in that heavily wooded area, the rangers and a few of the hikers carried the stretcher toward a clearing, with Janey walking alongside. Every few minutes she would ask that the litter be set down so that she could check Marianna's condition. "I'd tell her to look at me. I wanted to see if she could still hear me, and if she was conscious enough to open her eyes and understand what I was saying. I also wanted to check the size of her pupils and whether they were reacting to light. I remember so clearly the first time I asked her that. She opened her eyes and they were a really bright blue. That made such an impression on me, because she looked right at me with those big blue eyes."

When they reached a meadow that looked as though it would be a safe place for a helicopter to land, one of the seasonals who had worked with helicopters in the Army flagged the area. He placed bright pieces of clothing on the four corners of a space sufficiently wide for the aircraft to put down. As they waited, Janey gave Marianna more oxygen and checked the dressings. "We were just trying to keep her alive until the chopper got there with the doctor. There was nothing else we could do."

Marianna seemed to be losing her battle for life. She looked waxen, although amazingly enough, she was still conscious. Then, faintly, Janey heard the whirring of helicopter blades. Everyone jumped and waved as the aircraft came into view, hovered, and landed. A doctor and his aide leaped out to run to where Marianna lay. They took her blood pressure, but couldn't get any reading at all. Immediately they began to give her an intravenous solution. "She'd been on her way out," Janey says, "but when they started that I-V it was as though life flowed back into her again. I could see that she was coming back, and I was so glad. As soon as she was stabilized, we put her into the helicopter, still in the Stokes litter, and they flew her to Lake Hospital."

At the park's Lake Hospital, the doctor gave Marianna further treatment to prepare her for a flight to the University of Utah Medical Center in Salt Lake City, where she underwent five major operations during the next seven weeks. After her initial hospital stay, she returned at several-month intervals for further plastic surgery to repair the damage to her skin and muscles.

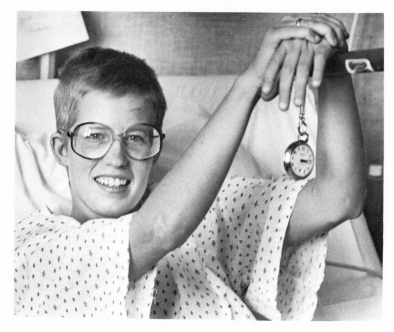

After seven weeks of intensive medical treatment to keep her alive, Marianna Young is ready to leave the hospital.

What about the bear? Was it hunted and destroyed?

"In a case like that," Janey explains, "the Park Service had to consider it a circumstance where the bear was protecting its young in the wilderness. Since a mothering instinct is natural for a wild animal, it would have been unjust to punish the bear. Even if we'd wanted to, we couldn't have been certain of finding the right bear because there are more than two hundred grizzlies in the park, plus several hundred black bears. Marianna's case was a tragic encounter between a human and a bear where no one was at fault, because the bear was acting the way it normally would in the wild."

Immediately after the mauling, though, the Heart Lake

area was closed and carefully patrolled for most of the summer to make certain that the grizzly wasn't frequenting the trail. When the area was opened again, it was limited to parties of four or more hikers.

"For most people," Janey says, "the only times they've seen real bears are at the zoo or the circus, where the bears look tame and friendly. But they're wild animals. If their space is intruded upon, they're probably going to get aggressive . . . , and it isn't just the bears who act that way, but all the other large animals as well."

Janey believes visitors to the park should be given a great deal of information about the animals and their behavior, a policy that is followed scrupulously. When visitors drive through the entrance stations, they receive pamphlets telling them about bears and other wild animals in Yellowstone, explaining the way the animals can be expected to act. They're also warned about the dangers of thermal pools.

"We're very much concerned about safety," Janey says. "We want everyone who comes here to have a safe and meaningful visit. But if we wanted to make Yellowstone totally and completely secure, we'd have to seal off all the thermal areas and move the animals outside the boundaries. That would destroy the flavor and purpose of the park."

She adds, "There's a certain amount of hazard in experiencing wilderness. If people cross-country ski, they have to know about the hazards of cold weather and avalanches. If they take pictures of wild animals, they have to know that if they get too close, the animals might charge to protect themselves and their young. If they hike in bear country, they should know about carrying 'bear bells.' When the bears hear the ringing, they know people are coming, and they generally stay out of the way. Yellowstone is here to allow people to explore a primitive environment. We must give visitors the option of taking these risks, at the same time in-

Two years after the bear mauling, Janey and Marianna meet again under happier circumstances.

forming them fully of any possible dangers so that they can make their decisions intelligently."

Marianna Young continues to love the wilderness. The summer after the mauling, she went back to Yellowstone to hike the trails. And the year after that, she returned as a summer employee, wearing the ranger uniform of a park technician.

Working at the South Entrance, Marianna handed out information packets that included bear-warning leaflets, though she rarely told park visitors what had happened to her. "If I saw someone who was going to go hiking alone, I really warned against it. I never came out and said, 'Well, I was mauled by a bear once when I was hiking alone' because I didn't want to totally ruin their trip. But I gave out some pretty powerful warnings."

## SPECIAL DUTIES

*T*he summer that began so dramatically with the rescue of Marianna Young ended with a brief change of scene for Janey.

In September, President Jimmy Carter vacationed in the Grand Teton National Park, which borders Yellowstone to the south, and the Special Activities Group was called to help with security. For six nights President Carter stayed at the Brinkerhoff Lodge on Jackson Lake Dam while Janey patrolled outside.

"The President's Secret Service agents formed the inner perimeter of security around the lodge," she recalls, "and our night shift of twelve rangers worked in a circle beyond them. I'd go to my post at eight every evening to stand guard, using my ears more than my eyes in the darkness. I didn't move around too much because if I did, the Secret Service agents got nervous. And I got nervous, because I didn't want them pointing their guns at me. Besides, if I walked around I couldn't hear anyone who might have been prowling through the bushes. That's what I was there for, to make sure there weren't any intruders."

Not only did she see no intruders during the entire six nights that she worked twelve hours at a stretch, but she didn't even see the President once. "That's the way it goes sometimes." Janey shrugs, adding with a grin, "I'm sure he enjoyed his stay in the Tetons even though he didn't get to meet me."

She'd been transferred to the South Entrance with the title of supervisory park ranger. The South Entrance is one of five gates through which visitors can drive into the park; the others are West, North, Northeast, and East. At a kiosklike building beside the road at the South Entrance, visitors pay two dollars for an entrance pass and receive information brochures about Yellowstone. Not far from the kiosk are houses and cabins where staff members live, an office, equipment storage buildings, and a stable and corral for the horses.

As her park experience and responsibilities increased, Janey found herself doing a lot more paperwork. Because she was spending more hours at a desk, she made a special effort to keep fit. Each day at dawn she put on a sweat suit and Adida shoes to run 6 miles along the trails, building up her stamina for any unexpected special duties. A job description for her new position stated: "Physical demands can be arduous. [The ranger] must routinely be able to handle heavy equipment such as chain saws, logs, bridge planks, etc. In emergencies, he or she must endure extreme physical exhaustion during forest fires, mountain or water rescues, or long searches in difficult terrain." Janey ran not only to keep herself in peak physical condition for just such emergencies, but also to steep herself in the beauty of the wilderness before beginning the day's press of work.

In the evenings she found relaxation by caring for the horses. In three minutes she could walk from her house at the South Entrance to the barn and corral, where four horses were quartered: Eli, who'd been Janey's favorite from the beginning; Jet; Chico; and Socks. She threw hay into a large trough for their evening feeding, then sat on the corral fence to watch the rose-colored sun lower to the surrounding pines. The horses would amble over to nudge her pockets

Evening conversation relaxes Janey and Socks.

with their soft noses, asking for the treats Janey always carried for them.

The horses were not ridden for pleasure. They were kept for boundary patrol or for packing supplies into the backcountry. In August 1979, Janey and a seasonal ranger named Michael traveled into the Heart Lake region to supply a ranger who'd been keeping fire lookout all through the summer. By a little past six in the morning Janey and Michael had loaded the gear and horses into a trailer, which they drove to the Heart Lake trail head. Early sunlight dappled the horse trailer with leaf shadows as the rangers packed Jet with supplies, then saddled Eli and Socks.

ABOVE: Caring for the horses is more pleasure than work.

BELOW: Janey and Michael pack Jet with supplies for the Heart Lake fire-watcher.

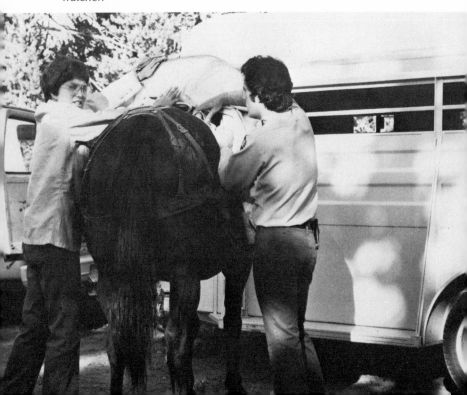

Their trip had an extra purpose: In addition to packing in groceries for Jim, the fire lookout, Janey would check the progress of a forest fire burning on the shore of Heart Lake. It was a "let burn" fire. Since it had started from a natural cause, lightning, no effort had been made to put it out. The rangers watched it closely, though, because it was burning fairly near one of the patrol cabins.

The first part of the ride was pleasant, but as Michael and Janey rode farther along, the sky above them grew hazy with thin smoke. When they stopped for a lunch break, they noticed an airplane flying in large circles overhead. They forgot about eating as they watched it circle. Suddenly two parachutes appeared beneath the plane, catching the air to open in wide orange hemispheres as they lowered men to the trees some distance away. Janey was surprised, but she assumed that for some reason smoke jumpers had been dropped to fight the Heart Lake fire.

For the next 3 miles the trail rose steeply along the side of Mount Sheridan, a hard climb for the horses. When Janey and Michael reached the summit, where they had a panoramic view of Heart Lake, they were startled by the intensity of the fire raging below them. "Just as we got there the fire started to really blow," Janey says. "Even though we were pretty far away from it, the heat was so intense that we could actually see flames leaping from tree to tree. Heavy black smoke hovered close to the trees; then as it rose it billowed up into a huge white cloud. We watched the fire 'spot' . . . it threw out flames several hundred feet in front of the main part of the blaze, flames that torched out whole trees in an instant."

After they'd found Jim and unloaded his supplies from Jet, the three of them sat on the side of the mountain to observe the fire's course. In late afternoon Michael and Janey rode down the trail to the ranger cabin where they would spend

The Heart Lake fire in Yellowstone

the night. By the time they'd fed and picketed the horses and cooked their own dinner, they could see thick gray smoke through the cabin windows. Although the fire was far enough away so that they were not in danger, its smoke blanketed an ever-widening area.

That night Jerry called on the radio to report that the two smoke jumpers had been dropped, not to fight the Heart Lake fire, but to quickly put out a small, visitor-caused blaze at a campsite some distance from the main fire. Janey and Michael were to meet the smoke jumpers the next morning and carry out their gear on Jet.

At dawn they started along the lake trail, riding through terrain that the large forest fire had burned earlier. "We went past several spots where we could see flames licking close to the ground about eight feet from the trail. They were just little flames, but the horses got kind of spooked, and the smoldering undergrowth was so smoky that our eyes hurt. We knew that the forest fire was not too far away, but we couldn't really see it, not the main part."

When they reached the campsite where the smoke jumpers were waiting, Janey and Michael loaded the men's gear onto Jet's back: two orange parachutes, jump suits, fire pumps, axes, and hoes. Although the small manmade fire had been put out promptly because it was in a camping area that many people used, the much larger nature-caused wilderness fire was allowed to burn. Visitors were not permitted anywhere near the danger area.

By autumn, when cool weather and rain put out the Heart Lake fire, it had covered 5,000 acres. That seems like a sizable area, yet it represents only one fourth of one percent of the total extent of Yellowstone. The acreage had been "let burn" because of a new policy that recognizes that fire, when it is not people-caused, is part of nature's way of renewing the forest.

# *Karen Eckels*

## WILDLAND FIRE SPECIALIST

*A*s Janey and Michael rode back from the fire in Yellowstone, Karen Eckels was studying wildfire information on a computer screen in Boise, Idaho. References on the use of fire in pinyon-juniper forests appeared one after the other on the screen. Mesa Verde National Park had requested that information only a few days before. Unlike the Heart Lake fire, which was a natural fire that was allowed to burn, the fire Mesa Verde Park was concerned with was one that park managers wanted to ignite themselves. By using fire under controlled conditions, they could get rid of built-up fuels and prevent a large destructive wildfire later. But before they could begin, they needed information from Karen's computer. It would tell them when a fire could safely be started, and how it would burn.

Working with capable assurance, Karen Eckels seems perfectly suited to her profession. But she arrived at it in a roundabout way, after a series of the coincidental twists and turns that occur in almost every person's life.

Karen is in frequent contact with resource agencies all over the country.

Born in Kingston, New York, Karen moved with her family to Salt Lake City, Utah, when she was five. Her parents bought a house in a new subdivision where few other homes had yet been built, but Karen wasn't lonely. She had her dark-haired sister, Nancy, two years older.

"For as long as I can remember," Karen says, "Nancy wanted to be an actress. Even when we were very small, we made up plays with costumes and props. Then, after Nancy started school, she taught me to read and write and work with numbers."

Because of this early tutoring, Karen skipped some semesters of school and graduated from high school when she was just sixteen. Ready to start college, she had no definite career goals in mind, but she enjoyed literature and writing, and had been editor of her high school yearbook. She enrolled as an English major at a college in Washington state.

After the first year, when Karen went home for summer vacation, a friend told her that the government employment service was hiring people for the Youth Conservation Corps. Karen applied and was accepted.

It was 1971 and the Youth Conservation Corps, just getting started, had opened its first sixty-four summer camps all over the United States. It had been set up by the Department of the Interior, the Department of Agriculture's Forest Service, and some state agencies in order to give fifteen-to-eighteen-year-olds a chance to learn about the environment. While learning, the young people would do constructive work and earn the minimum hourly wage. YCC positions were evenly divided among girls and boys, with the girls expected to do the same kinds of physical work as the boys. At some "residential" camps the crew members lived in tents, bunkhouses, or college dormitories; other enrollees lived at home and commuted to camp each day.

For ten weeks that summer, from Monday through Friday,

Karen lived at a YCC camp operated by the Forest Service not too far from her home. Most of the fifty corps members at the camp were high school students. Only Karen and one other girl had a year of college.

"We did a little bit of everything," Karen says. "We cut trees that had fallen along trails, cleared away brush, and planted new young trees. I remember an awful lot of painting that summer, mostly of Forest Service cabins. You wouldn't think log cabins would take so long to paint, but they must have twice as much surface area as anything else."

At least once a week the staff members gave environmental education programs—in which the young crew members experimented with soil or water or forest ecology. "One of the things they taught us," Karen recalls, "was water-testing—to see what kinds of organisms lived in the water and to figure out how big a city population one stream could support. We studied soil composition, too. It was fairly basic stuff, but a good, broad look at how things interrelate."

Since the region where they worked was ski country, the YCC members lived in a ski lodge, which would otherwise have been unused in the summer. High mountain peaks loomed above them, still snowcapped in the middle of July. The slopes were lined with tall dark pines. Here and there narrow stands of trees had been toppled by snow avalanches so that all their trunks pointed downhill, looking from a distance like spilled toothpicks.

As a college girl among high school students, Karen felt confined by the strict rules governing the crew members, but in some ways she was still a novice. "On my very first backpack trip," she says, "I was one of the worst-equipped. Fortunately it was a short hike, only about five miles. I was carrying a Dacron sleeping bag, which seemed heavy, even on the way to the campground. Then it rained like crazy that night and my sleeping bag got soaked. On the trip back it weighed about forty pounds. I couldn't wait to get it off my back." After that, Karen bought a much lighter, down-filled, bag.

In that first summer of the Youth Conservation Corps, 1,348 female crew members worked in camps throughout the country. By 1978, the corps gave jobs to 21,728 girls, and the program is still growing. Crew members of both sexes like the program. In surveys taken over the years, ninety-nine percent have said so, and Karen Eckels agrees.

Ten weeks of hard physical work in air that smelled of pine and pungent moss rather than exhaust fumes convinced Karen that she'd be happy with an outdoor career. She transferred to Colorado State with a major in wildlife biology, but something went wrong. Classwork was different from the kind of work she'd done on the mountain. Too many of the courses were preliminaries that had little to do with natural resources.

At that time her sister, Nancy, was studying acting in California. Nancy always had exciting stories to tell about the parts she played in summer theater. After only one quarter in wildlife biology, Karen changed her major—to drama, for the rest of the year.

Back in Utah again for the summer, Karen looked for a job to help with her college expenses. She found one as a sandwich maker in a little restaurant, but only hours before she was to report for the first time, she got a phone call from a man who'd been director of the YCC camp the summer before. There was an opening for a crew leader at the camp, he said, and it was hers if she wanted it.

"That was a turning point for me," Karen says. "I was so elated over the chance to get back into the mountains! Suddenly I realized that it didn't make sense for me to be studying theater, where the only place I could get ahead was in a big city. That night I decided I had made a big mistake getting out of the natural-resource field."

At the end of that summer, the camp director told Karen she was the best crew leader they'd had, because she related so well to the crew members. That was not so surprising. Karen was hardly older than the ten kids on her crew. "There were a lot of times when I didn't feel comfortable," she says. "We'd get to a job and I'd get out of the truck and say 'Let's go,' and the kids would say 'No.' On occasions like that I got a bit earthy with my language, and I usually let them know that I was serious."

Though Karen herself is tall, she found it tricky, even a little scary, to reprimand boys only a year younger who towered over her. She tried not to let her lack of confidence show. Even though supervisors weren't supposed to take shovel in hand and do the work (they were supposed to make sure that everyone else was working), Karen says, "Sometimes I had to get in there and dig in order not to have a rebellion on my hands. The kids needed to see that I wasn't afraid to work."

In spite of the few problems, Karen was more certain than ever that she wanted to work in natural resources. From camp she sent away for catalogs of colleges that offered forestry as a major. In one catalog from a university on the West Coast, she read that women could find satisfying careers in forestry as assistant researchers and assistant planners. "I didn't see why I should have to be an assistant anything," Karen declares. "Since I wanted to play a major role in whatever I did, I threw that particular catalog into the wastebasket."

She applied to the University of Montana in Missoula, and

only days before the autumn quarter was to begin, telephoned Missoula to learn whether she'd been accepted. She had. After enrolling in the University of Montana, Karen knew that she had at last found the place and the field where she belonged.

## THE FOREST SERVICE

*M*issoula was a pleasant university town set in the foothills of a Rocky Mountain range, but flat enough for Karen to ride her bike to class. Because of all the changes she'd made in her major, she would require three years of classwork to graduate from the university with a degree in forestry. But right from the start she had the kind of classes she wanted: wildlife biology, forest ecology, and studies of water and soil.

She liked Missoula so much that she decided to spend her summers there, and again was a crew leader for the Youth Conservation Corps, this time at an all-girl camp in the Lolo National Forest. It was an interesting contrast to the coed camps she'd attended previously.

"At the coed camps," Karen says, "the girls were afraid, at least at the beginning of the summer, to be seen with shovels in their hands because the boys might think them unfeminine. Most of them got over that, though. By the end of the summer, they were determined to show that they could do anything the boys could do."

At the all-girl Lolo Forest camp, the crew members never had to worry about how they looked to the opposite sex, and they turned out incredible amounts of work. Since the Forest Service wanted to know how participants felt about the camps, they polled the twenty-four corps girls at Lolo. Nearly all the girls said they preferred all-female enrollment.

They did heavy work thinning trees in the conifer forest. Although the younger girls were allowed to use only pruning shears, the eighteen-year-olds learned to handle heavy chain saws. Karen had few discipline problems. "There were times when we would walk over to the dormitory and find four or five girls being silly, sitting on the front porch smoking cigars," she says, "but we didn't consider that much of a problem."

Just before camp ended after Karen's second summer at Lolo National Forest, she and the other leaders took all the girls on a week-long backpack trip to an area of alpine

More women are being hired by the Forest Service, although they make up only 10 percent of the fire-fighting crews. These women learn about chain saws.

meadows and small, beautiful lakes. Having worked with them for nine weeks, the leaders thought the YCC girls were responsible enough to hike at their own pace and enjoy the scenery. "We didn't want them to feel too regimented," Karen says, "although they were all expected to stay on the same trail.

"By the third day," she continues, "we were literally in the middle of nowhere on the high ridge trail. When we reached our destination for the night, the camp director stood beside the trail to make certain everyone had arrived. I was one of the last to come in. He asked whether I'd seen two particular corps members, but I hadn't."

Karen and the camp director waited in the gathering darkness, straining to hear any footfalls on the path. No one approached. With growing concern, they had to admit that the two girls were probably lost.

Since it was so dark, the camp director decided against sending out crew members to search for them. That would be too dangerous. The searchers would only get lost too. With a hand radio he called fire lookouts who were stationed atop high towers along the trail, alerting them about the missing campers. The lookouts radioed Forest Service headquarters to request a helicopter at daylight. Everyone spent an anxious night waiting for the first streaks of dawn to lighten the sky.

Unknown to Karen and the other crew leaders, the two missing girls had wandered off the high ridge trail and had kept on walking until they found another trail at the bottom of a canyon. At first neither of them realized that they were lost, although they did wonder why they weren't meeting any other hikers from the group. They stayed on the lower trail for miles until they arrived, worn-out and cold, at the shore of a lake. There they found a party of good-hearted campers who offered to share their tent for the night so the girls could stay dry. Leaving their backpacks on the ground outside, they went inside the tent to sleep.

When they woke in the morning, the two girls found that their backpacks had been slashed by bears. All their freeze-dried food was gone and their clothes were strewn everywhere. If they had not slept inside that tent, they might have been in serious danger.

"For some reason, and I can't imagine why," Karen says, "at that point they decided to go swimming in the lake. While they were in the water the search helicopter circled overhead looking for them, but because it was foggy and they were mostly covered by lake water, the pilot missed seeing them."

Meanwhile, Karen and the other leaders were hurrying the rest of the girls toward the same lake, where they'd planned all along to camp the following night. They wanted to get the group deposited in one place while the professional searchers did their job, rather than have nearly two dozen girls strung out along the trail to confuse searchers.

Before they got there, the helicopter pilot returned to the lake to make a few more passes along the shoreline. This time he spotted the missing girls and radioed that they were safe. Soon everyone was reunited: the lost campers embarrassed but joyful, the other girls wide-eyed over the bear-slashed backpacks, and the YCC leaders relieved that the episode had ended without tragedy.

"On the way back from the campout," Karen remembers, "those kids were *really* regimented!"

By the middle of August the girls went home from the YCC camp and Karen changed jobs, doing a different kind of work until classes started in late September. Still a seasonal employee of the Forest Service, she worked at what people usually envision when they hear the term "forest ranger."

Early each morning, Karen joined a crew of eight (the rest men), who studied timber habitat in the Lolo National Forest. The Forest Service had sent out planes to take aerial photographs of the area; from the photos they divided the mountains into "stands"—small units of forested land with uniform natural features. Every day Karen's crew received a map of the different stands they were to study.

"In late August the weather was still nice," Karen says, "but by September it got cold up on those mountains. As we drove to the stands where we were to work, we always pulled in at a truck stop to fill our thermos bottles with hot coffee."

When they reached the work area, the crew members carried 6-foot poles to measure the ground. Walking in a straight line for 66 feet, eleven pole lengths, they stopped to take a "plot" sampling, holding the pole straight out as they pivoted in a circle. The orbit of the pole's outer tip marked the circumference of the plot to be sampled.

Karen and the others then counted the trees in the plot and recorded their species, their heights, and whether the trunks showed any signs of insect damage or fire-scarring.

Some of the plots were thickly covered with foot-high seedling trees, that had either grown naturally or been planted a year earlier by Forest Service crews. Because the Lolo Mountains are very dry in the summer, the seedlings often didn't survive. "They just couldn't hang on without moisture," Karen says. "In one area we found tree after tree dead . . . those poor little trees only ten inches high had just dried up, hundreds of them. I found maybe one live one among a hundred dead ones."

Other areas were growing quite well, and by late autumn were actually too wet for Karen's comfort. "There's a particular type of plant called menziesia," she says, "that has leaves which seem shaped just to hold water. After a rain-

The September snow edged Karen's hair as she checked the condition of trees in the high mountains.

storm or after the first snows had melted, the menziesia bushes would be waiting to douse us. And of course they grow about head high. I'd take ten steps through that growth and I'd be soaked from head to foot."

At the end of the timber habitat season it got downright cold, snowing often, but it was a pleasant, crisp cold, and the snow-covered mountains looked beautiful. Karen and the others would walk five or six abreast, in a 66 foot line, leaving fresh tracks in the newly fallen snow. Stopping in a straight line to call out the trees on the plots, they saw each word create its own wreath of vapor. "At least we could wear gloves," Karen says, "but the guy in the middle, who had to write down all the data, nearly froze his hands."

After the whole crew got thoroughly chilled and snow-covered, they dashed for the truck, piling inside and pouring coffee from thermoses held in shivering hands. "We'd be all smashed together," Karen remembers, "squeezing the coffee cups for warmth. After being so cold outside, it felt great to huddle together in that truck. The windows would fog up fast because we were all so wet."

Karen wore jeans, a yellow hard hat, and layers of clothes: T-shirt, heavy work shirt, and down-filled vest. No long underwear, though. "I never knew how the weather was going to turn out," she explains. "If it warmed up, as it did often, I didn't want to run and look for a place where I could hide from the men while I got my longjohns off."

Because all living things, including trees, have a life cycle that ends with old age and disease, the Forest Service monitors the condition of the trees throughout all national forests. When a stand of trees has reached its peak growth and would begin to decline from then on, it may be offered to lumbering companies for harvesting. Loggers bid on the stand, naming sums of money based on the number of board feet they think can be sawed from the trees. Then, with the blessings of the Forest Service, they cut the trees, following rigid guidelines to protect the environment. Afterward they clear debris from the area. Usually early in the following spring, new seedlings are planted in the cleared area, either by the loggers themselves or by Forest Service crews and Youth Conservation Corps members.

Karen's work was a preliminary study called habitat-typing. It examined the stage of growth of the various stands. On the basis of information she and the other crew members provided, Forest Service managers knew whether a stand would be ready to harvest in a year, or not for another ten years. If the stand showed signs of having reached its peak, a second crew of "timber cruisers" would be sent to make an estimate of board feet to compare against the logging company's later offer. The timber-cruising crew checked trees for condition as well as size. A fir tree with a forked top, for instance, won't produce as much lumber as one with a single, thicker top. Then they marked the stand for harvesting. In some cases they went through a stand and marked only certain trees to be cut.

Forest Service lands aren't used only for commercial logging, but because of logging the agency got its start. As is so often the case, federal control became necessary because private individuals were abusing the land. In the nineteenth century, so much original forestland was stripped for logging and farming that erosion and floods followed, causing a lot of damage. Forest fires raged and destroyed valuable timber.

To correct these abuses, the Forest Service was established by an act of Congress in 1905, and during the next few years the government set aside vast tracts of timberland for national forests. Fire control was the biggest priority of the early foresters, but they also helped farmers to plant trees to keep topsoil from blowing away.

Today the Forest Service has much broader goals. The 188 million acres of national forest are used for outdoor recreation, wildlife and fish habitat, cattle and sheep-grazing, and water protection. And, of course, for timber production.

The demand for wood and wood products has grown so phenomenally in the past few years that the value of lumber trees skyrocketed. Karen says, "Old growth ponderosa pines have an enormous value today because the trees are large and straight, and a single tree will produce a lot of lumber. But we have to be careful about harvesting them because when ponderosas grow in very dry areas, they're sometimes hard to reestablish after cutting. Our timber resources will last for future generations only if we're cautious about forest management."

## FINDING A JOB

When Karen Eckels graduated from the University of Montana, she expected to be hired as a full-time forester by the Forest Service. But much to her dismay, she learned that she wasn't qualified. She'd earned her degree in forestry with honors, but according to Civil Service (now the Office of Personnel Management) requirements, she hadn't taken enough classes in timber management.

A government official advises, "College students should be forewarned about federal job requirements. These kids go along taking courses specified by universities for degrees in forestry or recreation or wildlife, or whatever, thinking they'll get federal jobs when they graduate. Then they find out they don't have the right kind of background for government jobs at the professional level. It's a big blow when the Civil Service won't recognize their degrees." Each college student planning a career in a government agency should have counseling from the beginning, the official advises, to tailor coursework to federal standards. "If you haven't taken the right courses, you don't get hired."

Karen considered going back to the university to take additional classes in timber studies, but she'd already spent five years in college, and she felt it was time to be employed at something besides a summer vacation job. Though she couldn't be hired as a forester, Karen hoped another government opening might come along. She took the Professional

Administrative Careers Examination—the PACE exam given by the Civil Service. On its six sections she scored three 99s and three 100s. Then, because she needed an immediate salary, she signed up again as a Youth Conservation Corps leader.

Toward the end of that summer in the Lolo Forest, Karen learned that she'd qualified for a position with the Forest Service in the Northern Forest Fire Laboratory in Missoula, a center for research on wildfire behavior. In its 66-foot-high combustion chamber, fuels are burned directly underneath a funnel-bottomed cylinder that looks like an enormous stovepipe. Scientists ignite fuel beds of grass or twigs or pine needles while they control the temperature, humidity, and atmospheric pressure in the chamber to learn how hot and how fast fuels will burn under different weather conditions.

Next to the combustion chamber is a wind tunnel that looks like a long, high, square-sided folding telescope. Artificial winds of up to 50 miles an hour can be produced inside this tunnel and a smaller one like it. When fires are lit inside the tunnels, scientists discover how flames behave in winds of different speeds. Although the test fires are much smaller than real forest fires would be, the test results often are verified in small, controlled forest fires deliberately set around Missoula. Based on the results of these experiments, forest managers can make informed decisions about fire management and fire suppression.

Karen's job was in an office, a very tiny, crowded office, because there wasn't much space left in the laboratory buildings. It involved reading articles and documents about wildfire, condensing the information into short abstracts, and storing the abstracts in a computer memory bank. She was hired as a temporary employee on a one-year contract.

"The first day I was pretty apprehensive," Karen says, "because I'd never before had a job where I needed to perform intellectually rather than just dig a trail or supervise kids. My boss handed me an article and said, 'Abstract this, and when you get through I'll tell you whether you've done it right.' " For hours Karen sat there, reading the document and wondering what she was supposed to do with it.

Weeks passed before she began to understand the difference between literary writing and technical writing. Her supervisor had been trained as a journalist, and was used to condensing a lot of information in a few words. But as a former English major, Karen had studied literature. "My problem," she says, "was that I wanted all my work to sound like a great masterpiece. In abstracting, you don't flower up the language with phrases like 'the miracle of modern computers.' You just say 'computers' and let it go at that. I thought I was being creative, using lots of adjectives and sentences that were four lines long."

Her boss was patient, and within three months Karen could read a document and condense the important information in it. The documents were articles from journals written by professionals concerned with fire research—foresters, fire fighters, and university researchers. Just as Karen was getting good at abstracting, she was transferred to another phase of the work.

Fire-fighting data had been stored in a computer. This information was listed under random key words, words that were fed into the machine to retrieve the information. Documents about fire retardants, for example, might be indexed under "chemical fire suppressants," under "fire retarding chemicals," or "airdropped fire retardants," and many more. The computer wasn't smart enough to know that all those key words were about the same subject, so the index had to be made uniform. For months Karen plowed through a huge stack of papers to list all the titles under nine hundred terms, cross-referenced.

"Airdropped fire retardants," "chemical fire suppressants," "fire retarding chemicals"—these key words had to be indexed under one title for the computer.

"By then it was summer," Karen remarks, "the first summer I hadn't worked out in the open. I just gazed out the window, wishing I could be back in the mountains." That summer she made five weekend and vacation trips to Glacier National Park in northern Montana to smell the fresh mountain air and walk among the giant fir trees again.

Just as Karen's one-year job contract ended, the eighteen-month research phase of the project was completed, too. The program had been named Firebase, and it was ready to operate. Instead of finding herself out of work, Karen learned that she'd been chosen to run the whole program, but not in Missoula. Firebase and Karen Eckels were moving to Boise, Idaho.

## FIREBASE

*F*irebase was all set to work, providing information about wildland fires to anyone who asked for it. The system was now located in the Boise Interagency Fire Center. Karen would work not only for the Forest Service, but also for the Bureau of Land Management, the National Park Service, the Bureau of Indian Affairs, and the Fish and Wildlife Service. These agencies cooperated to suppress wildfires all over the United States.

Karen says, "I thought that in Boise I was going to do pretty much the same kinds of things I'd done in Missoula. When I got there I found out that the program manager didn't have any technical knowledge about Firebase, and the responsibility fell to me."

Karen knew a lot about writing abstracts, but next to nothing about operating a computer terminal. What saved her was her complete knowledge of the information stored in the computer, and her familiarity with the key-word vocabulary she'd put together. "If I punched some key words into the computer terminal, and the right information didn't come out and I knew it was in there, I could go back and redo it or figure out what I'd done wrong." Karen had a very short time to learn to operate the computer, though. Only a week after she began work in Boise, she was sent to a large professional meeting to demonstrate Firebase.

It was then that Karen became grateful for her varied college background. The Firebase job required writing skills to prepare abstracts: Karen had been an English major for a year. It required a forestry background: Karen certainly had that, even though the Civil Service didn't consider her qualified to be a forester. And she needed the ability to talk about the new program before audiences of professional people: The two quarters she'd spent as a drama major gave her the poise for public appearances. Education is never wasted, Karen decided.

With her portable computer terminal, she arrived at a joint conference of the Society of American Foresters and the American Meteorological Society, held in Saint Louis. She was given a room where she could set up her equipment and display some printouts that she'd made in advance "in case I couldn't get the computer to work." Firebase was a new product and she had to promote it, convincing the foresters and meteorologists that they could save a lot of time by letting Firebase search out information for them.

Karen had never attended a conference like that one, let alone made a speech at one. Her demonstration wasn't a regularly scheduled part of the program—it was announced at the end of the first day's meeting. When she heard the chairperson's announcement, Karen's heart sank. In a room filled with three hundred men and only one other woman, he said, "We brought Karen Eckels here with us because she's a member of the Society of American Foresters . . . and because she's pretty." Almost as an afterthought he added, "She's going to give a demonstration in the room next door."

The compliment was probably intended innocently enough, but Karen didn't appreciate it. She wanted the delegates to attend her demonstration because she had something important to present, not because of her looks. As a result of the chairperson's quip, she felt that the demonstration was taken less seriously than it should have been. A few men dangled their hotel keys and joked, "Why don't you stop up and see me afterward?" Or, "If you're the one who's

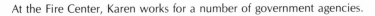

At the Fire Center, Karen works for a number of government agencies.

going to answer the phone when I call Firebase, I'll call every week."

"It's not that they were trying to be obnoxious," Karen believes, "it's more a case that they didn't know how to relate to me. I know I was young, twenty-three at the time, but I was doing a good job with the demonstrations. The computer *was* working properly, and I conducted searches on information people had requested right while they were standing there." Though disappointed by the banter of some of her listeners, Karen didn't complain to the chairperson, because "at the time I was too spineless."

That changed a year later. Karen had gone to a number of conferences by that time to make people aware of Firebase. She taught a course in the use of the system at a fire-training center near Tucson, Arizona, and then was sent to repeat the course in Chevy Chase, Maryland. There she was to show that Firebase could be useful for eastern fire-fighting, where conditions are very different from those in the West.

As usual, Karen was the only woman on the fire-prevention cadre at Chevy Chase. Before the meeting began, the trainers and trainees talked together, becoming acquainted. Karen introduced herself to one of the men, saying, "I'm not one of the trainees. I'm part of the program."

"Oh? What are you going to do?" he asked. "Dance?"

Seething, Karen decided that she wasn't going to go through another experience like the one in Saint Louis. She looked for the man who would make the introductions. "I buttonholed him beforehand," Karen says, "and I told him, 'Now I want a straight introduction—no crap!'"

She thought she'd been forceful enough, but the man evidently didn't believe her. He ended his introduction with, "Karen Eckels . . . you'll really like her blue eyes." And when he introduced the next man on the team, he said, "Now this guy *really* likes blue eyes!"

"I didn't see why I should have to be an assistant anything," Karen concluded during her college years

KAREN ECKELS
HEAD FIREBASE LADY

KAREN ECKELS

Karen was no longer as spineless as she'd been the year before. "I was not going to put up with that sort of unprofessional put-down," she says. "He didn't make any sort of garbage comments like that about any of the men. I not only told him what I thought, I let several other people know what had happened. It even ended up in a written report that we objected to the way he conducted that introduction."

Younger men, Karen notes, are not nearly as condescending in their attitudes toward her. It's the men who have been working in the agencies since long before women were hired to do nontraditional professional work who don't know how to accept women in managerial roles. Like Janey McDowell, Karen grew more confident as her experience increased.

As a result of her instructive appearances, more and more users requested data from Firebase. Additional information was fed into the system, increasing its value to users. As word of the data bank spread, requests for information came not only from the United States, but from all parts of the world. The following diligently translated letter arrived from the Netherlands:

*"We like to ask you to help us collect bibliographic information concerning:*
*'Prevention of forest fires by sheep'*
*We hope that your Firebase contains information about this subject. We searched by all our own information centres in the databases available.*
*If there are any costs, we will pay. We must have collected this information before the end of February 1980.*
*We hope you can help us!"*

Karen comments, "They certainly did a better job of asking the question in English than I would if I had to answer it in Dutch."

The question about sheep had to do with fuel breaks— wide paths cut through forests as fire barriers. If a burning tree falls into a cleared fuel break, the fire has nothing to feed on and goes out. In pine forests in the southern United States, new vegetation grows rapidly in cleared areas, so sheep are allowed to graze on the new growth to keep the fuel breaks clear.

Karen usually mailed out answers to questions like this within three days after she received the requests. More complex answers, such as those about letting fires burn, might take a bit longer.

For years all forest fires were suppressed. Because of the belief that the nation's resources had to be preserved, the Forest Service and other agencies followed a policy of strict fire control. In the 1970s, that policy began to change. To-day, in specially designated areas, fires that are started by lightning may be allowed to burn to prevent larger future fires.

How can fires prevent fires? Because of the way fuel col-lects. Pine needles and branches fall to the forest floor. The more crowded the trees are, the faster this happens. Shrubs growing in the understory lose their leaves every autumn. Trees grow old, die, and crash to earth. In wet forests, this fallen material decays, but where the climate is dry, the dead vegetation accumulates into tons of fuel per acre. If fires don't sweep through every few decades to clear away the debris with a light surface burn, fuel builds up to dan-gerous levels. Then, when a wildland fire does start, it ex-plodes into a hot conflagration that is almost impossible to control.

Officials of national parks, national forests, and public rangelands have found certain areas where the environment can be better managed by allowing some fires to burn under predetermined conditions. Taking into account the kinds of trees, their heights and ages, the kind of ground cover and the amount of debris on the forest floor, officials decide in advance how severe a fire would be if it got started in a particular area in various kinds of weather. The officials then write a fire-management plan, spelling out, area by area, whether a blaze will be suppressed if it starts or be allowed to burn, depending on weather and fuel conditions.

Firebase supplies valuable data for the framing of these fire-management plans. Research results from the Northern Forest Fire Laboratory in Missoula and other research labs are sent on request, along with existing fire-management plans written for other parks or forests. A plan prepared for one zone may be useful as a reference for an identical zone in another area. This saves the cost of duplicating research.

Fire plans are flexible enough to be altered for changing conditions at the time of the blaze. On June 29, 1976, lightning struck a 50-foot spruce tree in Yellowstone National Park. Fuels on the ground around it immediately started to burn. The fire began halfway up a slope covered with spruce and lodgepole—since heat travels upward, fires on hills spread faster than fires on flat land. Because winds were light, the plan indicated that the fire should be allowed to burn. It was watched closely, though.

Spreading slowly, the fire had burned four acres by the first of July. Elk grazing in a meadow below seemed undisturbed by it, but park visitors on a road overlooking the slope stopped their cars to ask rangers what the smoke was.

RIGHT: In a modern adaptation of the old-fashioned bucket brigade, a helicopter transports lake water to drop on flames.

LEFT: In certain areas the environment can be better managed by allowing some fires to burn, under predetermined conditions.

Then, on July 2, winds became stronger and the fire flared, leaping from treetop to treetop over 30 acres. The elk moved away to safer ground, and traffic snarled as visitors jumped out of their cars to watch the drama. Park officials reconsidered the "let burn" decision, mostly because the fire was spreading close to electric power lines, and a power shutoff would cause major problems on the Fourth of July weekend. They decided to call in fire crews to put out the blaze.

Fire fighters pumped water from a small stream below the slope while additional water was being dropped from a large bucket suspended beneath a helicopter. The helicopter flew to the nearest lake, dipped down to lower the bucket into the water, then flew back to the fire; a sophisticated adaptation of the old-fashioned bucket brigade. A week later, the last "smokes" were out.

Although that particular fire plan had been written before Firebase began operating, planning is still going on for other public lands. Firebase makes it easier. Many factors have to be considered: the steepness of mountains and the kinds of vehicles that can climb them, possible danger to people and buildings, the effect on wildlife if animals' homes are destroyed, and dozens of other circumstances. By the end of 1980, Firebase had that information in the six thousand documents stored in its computer.

When Karen Eckels first began working for the Forest Service, she was out in the open among green growing things. Now she works in an office, compiling and presenting information about fires, the greatest threat to the living forest. At times she remembers her days in the forest with a certain longing, which can be perceived in this journal entry she wrote during the autumn of 1980:

*"Although working with YCC groups was at times frustrating and discouraging, on the whole, the summers I spent as a crew leader with the program were the best I've enjoyed. I remember one day in particular that brings back everything I loved about working and living in the woods.*

*"It was another of our long backpack trips into the mountains that run the state line between Idaho and Montana. Three days earlier we had started in from Hoodoo Pass, and were now a good twenty-five miles from anywhere. We had just finished eating lunch at a small lake tucked at the base of a ridge and surrounded by wildflowers. Most of the group had already hoisted their packs and headed down the trail. Another member of the camp staff, one enrollee, and I were as usual lagging behind. The three of us had become close friends, and we shared a common philosophy about hiking: if you get where you're going by dinner time, you've hiked fast enough.*

*"As we left the lake, the trail angled steeply up and to the right, to a point where it crossed the ridge and disappeared. The sun was warm, but moderated by a cool breeze—perfect strolling weather. As we neared the ridge top, the vegetation along the trail began to change. We soon found ourselves in the midst of a prolific huckleberry patch. From the top of the ridge we could see for miles—the lake we had just come from and the colorful valley below, and the trail ahead dotted with the disappearing figures of our group as they widened the gap between us.*

*"To walk past such an idyllic setting was more than we could manage. We dropped our packs by the side of the trail and fell back against them. Handfuls of the plumpest huckleberries were within reach without sacrificing a comfortable position. And so we stayed, savoring huckleberries, sometimes dozing, talking only occasionally, each one pursuing her own thoughts, content in the warmth of the sun and secure in our feeling of companionship."*

Those times in the open were a special, unforgettable part of Karen's life. But to secure professional advancement, she had to move on, and she now finds much satisfaction in her work with Firebase. It's a national-level program. Karen is contributing on a much larger scale by providing information to people who are still out in the field doing the work and making the decisions.

Karen says, "It's not so much that I tell people, 'Fire management is changing now, and we no longer put out all fires.' What I do say to the land managers is, 'You have a professional responsibility to be as well-informed as you can when you're deciding whether to let a fire burn or suppress it.' That's the kind of service Firebase performs, providing information which is the basis of those decisions."

## THE BOISE INTERAGENCY FIRE CENTER

*T*he Fire Center where Karen works is located right next to the Boise airport. Though the center owns two helicopters and four air tankers, at the height of the fire season additional planes have to be leased from commercial airlines to transport all the fire fighters and equipment. When fire season starts, aircraft of every size and description land and take off only minutes apart, their sides painted with the names of Hughes Air West or American or United. Busy in her office, Karen has grown so used to the sound of helicopters and roaring jets that she rarely notices the flight activity.

In July and August, when fire season peaks, two thousand fire fighters may be funneled through the center in a single day. Crews are brought in from states in which fire danger is minimal and flown to places where fires have grown too big for local crews to handle.

Fire fighters are outfitted at the center's warehouse, an enormous building that holds the biggest supply of fire equipment in the world. Each crew member receives a basic fire pack: a yellow fire-resistant shirt, a hard hat, and work gloves. Paper sleeping bags and collapsible cardboard latrines are sent to the fire sites, where they're used and afterward burned, which is more economical than transporting standard ones back to Boise and sanitizing them.

In one room of the warehouse, smoke jumper suits hang

At the Center, smoke jumper
suits hang in rows like
lifeless astronauts.

on a rack—wire-mesh-visored helmets above metallic-fabric jackets above pants of the same material—looking like a row of lifeless astronauts. Another room has tables long enough for parachutes to be stretched out from top to harness. After they've been mended (the nylon cloth is often torn by tree limbs when smoke jumpers land) the parachutes are re-packed with great care. Smoke jumpers' lives depend on properly packed parachutes. At a special training area on the Fire Center grounds, smoke jumpers practice falling, dangling in harnesses suspended from cables rather than from actual parachutes.

Tremendous amounts of supplies are required for the thousands of fire personnel who may be working at a single forest fire. Hardworking crew members really need the three substantial meals a day that are set up on long tables inside tents. They also need equipment to fight the fires—planes to drop fire retardant, shovels, bulldozers, axes, and pumps have to be freighted into areas that may be hard to reach and almost roadless, and they must be there as soon as the crews arrive. Cooks, dispatchers, and first-aid people are on the scene, along with specialists who drive trucks with mobile fire-weather units to keep track of wind and weather on an hourly basis.

"Winds are the trickiest things to deal with," Karen says. "They cause the kind of blowups that kill people. A sudden shift of wind will change the direction of the fire and the speed at which it's burning."

At Idaho's 1979 Ship Island fire, two fire crewmen were working on the side of a creek opposite the main burn when the fire "spotted"—shot burning embers across the creek. Flames raced up the hill where the men were standing.

They knew they couldn't outrun the fire, so they got out the fire shelters crew members are required to carry folded and attached to their belts. These small, igloo-shaped shelters are made of material that looks like aluminum foil of a very heavy gauge. The insides are lined with fiberglass and have straps for the hands and feet. Fire fighters can flip open the shelters in about fifty seconds; then they lie on the ground with the domed shelters covering them, holding onto them with the straps.

Fire shelters work because of the way fires normally behave. In a light, fast-moving, but not intense, surface fire, the area around a particular tree may flame for only three or four minutes. Grass and leaves and pine needles flash quickly, then the fire moves on.

The ground beneath an aluminum fire shelter is cooler than the air above it, and the oxygen supply is greater next to the ground. Since an aluminum shelter can withstand heat of 400 or 500 degrees, the person underneath one should be able to survive until the fire travels past.

Smoke jumpers practice rappelling, a useful maneuver for getting out of trees they might land in.

One of the two men caught in the Ship Island fire was saved by his fire shelter, but the second man, for some reason, wasn't wearing his heavy work gloves. When the hand straps grew too hot for him to hold, he let go. Wind lifted the shelter, and the man died of heat and suffocation.

More fire fighter fatalities have occurred in California than in any other state because the fuels there are high in oils, which make them flash, and because the weather is so unpredictable. Hot, dry desert winds reach high speeds in California. They blow for a long time, then suddenly change course to push the flames in different directions. "When southern California starts to burn," Karen says, "it burns violently. Fire policy states that fires must be fought when they endanger property or lives, and too many Californians build quarter-of-a-million-dollar houses out in the middle of dry brush. Vast numbers of people have to go there to fight fires every summer."

When the Santa Ana winds turn California into a huge bonfire, the Boise Interagency Fire Center erupts with activity. Fresh fire crews, some from as far away as the East Coast, arrive to be outfitted and sent to the fires. Weary and exhausted crews return to rest, to be resupplied (sometimes the soles of their boots have burned through) and sent out again. Ordinance people contact restaurants and food dealers to look for fast additional sources of food, then lease trucks and airplanes that can transport personnel and equipment to all the burn areas in the western states. Most important, they must quickly assemble thousands of fire fighters.

Only in the past ten years have women been allowed to actually fight fires; they now make up about ten percent of the Forest Service crews. On temporary crews recruited from Indian tribes, the percentage of women is much higher.

Fire fighters can be quickly mustered on Indian reservations, perhaps because unemployment is high· among Indi-

American Indians are experts at fighting fires in dry areas. This woman's hard hat, fire-retardent shirt, and heavy gloves are required clothing in a fire camp.

ans and the crew members are well paid. American Indians make excellent fire fighters. They're used to outdoor work and are knowledgeable about forests. Since they usually live in arid regions, Indians know how to handle fires where the water supply is scarce.

In dry areas, surface fires are fought on the forest floor with fire lines (trenches) dug around the burn and with retardant dumped from airplanes. But if a hot, dry wind is blowing, fire not only spreads along the ground, it leaps across the tops of trees as well.

"At that point there's no way to contain it," Karen says. "You just wait for it to burn itself out, hoping that rain or snow will soon fall." Fire crews still battle valiantly to keep such fires from spreading to danger areas, but weather conditions determine that the fire will not be suppressed. The Heart Lake fire in Yellowstone stopped after burning 5,000 acres, which seems like a large area. By contrast, two Alaskan fires in the same year consumed 57,000 and 73,000 acres respectively.

In the past, the majority of forest fires were caused by people, careless campers who didn't put out their fires, by cigarettes, sparks from cars or trains, children playing with matches, or arson. With public education, the number of people-caused fires decreased dramatically.

Today half of all forest fires are caused by lightning, especially the dry lightning that strikes in the West and is not followed by rain. Clouds can be so high that raindrops evaporate before reaching the ground. A severe thunder-and-lightning storm can start a dozen fires simultaneously. Lightning strikes may smolder for days, and then, when conditions become right, begin to spread. If these lightning-caused fires do not threaten to cause much damage, they may be permitted to burn.

Light surface fires don't harm trees greatly because tree trunks are often fire-resistant. Thick bark on a ponderosa pine or western larch tree insulates the core of the tree, protecting it from damage. Fire can even help the tree by destroying insects that bore into its bark. Ponderosas benefit additionally from fire because it gives them the space they need to thrive, and fire helps lodgepole pine in an ingenious way.

The cones of one variety of lodgepole pine are sealed by secretions of pitch. Only after they've been heated enough by fire for the pitch to melt will the cones open to drop their seeds. This is also true of jack-pine cones, which has led to an unusual problem with a species of endangered bird called the Kirtland warbler.

Kirtland warblers nest only under low-hanging branches of young jack pines. After the pines grow so tall that their branches no longer shelter the nests, the warblers move to a new young stand. In Michigan, where the Kirtland warbler is protected, stands of old jack pines are burned every five years, allowing new seeds to be released and sprout so that the birds can find young trees with low branches. This burning policy is named Operation Popcone.

After fire clears a land area, the vegetation that comes up the following spring is different from the kind that grew there before the fire. Grass seeds blow in first. When the grass grows, it provides shade for germinating shrubs and flowers—sagebrush, larkspur, locoweed and others—so that their tiny starts don't dry out. These plants, as they grow, provide shade for seedling trees, and the original vegetation starts to return to the area. Usually the burned area is covered with prefire types of vegetation within ten years after a fire, and the new trees are in young, healthy condition.

## THE AUGUST INFERNO

*T*he chief of the United States Forest Service described 1979 as one of the worst fire seasons on record. By the end of the first week of August, major fires were burning in Montana, California, Wyoming, Oregon, and Nevada. The most violent fires blazed in Idaho, where it seemed to some people that half the state was going up in flames.

At Gallagher Peak, 40 miles northwest of Idaho Falls, a fire that began after a lightning strike on July 6 exploded into fury at the beginning of August, when high winds fanned it out of control. Fire crews struggled to dig lines around its 36,000 acres of burning brush.

At the same time, the Ship Island fire, where the crew member had been killed when he couldn't hold onto his fire shelter, spread to 10,000 acres.

Just 30 miles south of Ship Island, a far worse fire was raging at Mortar Creek along the Salmon River, close to where Janey McDowell had guarded Jimmy Carter on his presidential visit. "There's no force on earth powerful enough to cope with what we're seeing here," said Gordon Stevens, fire boss on the Mortar Creek fire. He added, "Nature will have to do her thing"—put out the fire by sending rain.

But in the following days humidity dropped as 35-mile-an-hour winds sprang up to whip the flames. Two thousand weary men and women who had been fighting the fire for days were joined by five hundred fresh crew members flown in from the Southern states. Only ten "burned out" crews were allowed to return to Boise for a rest. Everyone else was desperately needed to fight the inferno, which then covered 50,000 acres.

"It's a monster," the fire boss said about Mortar Creek. Crews set backfires to stop the advancing flames. Just the *backfires* set to control this one huge conflagration were bigger than most of the forty other fires then burning throughout the West. But the backfires didn't help. Winds fanned the flames so fast that officials were afraid to send fire fighters downwind of the blaze. "The canyons are so steep and the smoke . . . so dense that we couldn't even see what was happening on the north side of the fire," explained Dale Dufour, a spokesperson for the National Forest Service. "We couldn't plan escape routes. The whole canyon would go up in flames before we could get any of our people out." At

Weather is an important factor in fire control. At the Fire Center, the nation's weather is constantly monitored on these computers.

one point the fire was burning 18,000 acres a day, jumping the middle fork of the Salmon River in several locations.

Then, on Sunday, August 12, unexpected rain began to fall on all the Western fires, raising the morale of seven thousand fire fighters, half the nation's total force, who had been working eighteen-hour days. "Our forecasts just didn't call for this much rain or this heavy ground cover . . . this steady drip, drip is wonderful!" exulted Dufour. "The rain is light but steady, the best kind to have in this situation. It doesn't put out the fire, but it keeps it from spreading."

The rain cooled or stopped all the other forest fires, but not Mortar Creek. There it grounded aircraft and helicopters that had been moving supplies and fire fighters to the burning area. Fire crews had to lead pack mules up the steep canyons as they continued to build fire lines. Meanwhile, fire officials reorganized crews and supplies that had been taken off the cooling fires, transporting some of the people to Mortar Creek. By the time that fire was finally "controlled," which means that it was diminishing inside the fire lines, it had burned 65,300 acres of timber and rangeland.

Remarkably, in all the August fires, which consumed a total of 170,000 acres in six Western states before rains put them out or allowed them to be controlled, only one fire fighter lost his life, the man at Ship Island. Many other crew members were injured, mostly with sprained ankles, torn ligaments, and muscle damage. Some were injured when the fire's violent disruption caused rocks to dislodge and roll down on the crews. A woman fire fighter had to be rushed to medical care when she suffered a miscarriage. Had the Forest Service known she was pregnant, she would never have been allowed on the fire lines.

Half a year later, in February 1980, three Idaho men were charged with starting the Mortar Creek fire. A lawsuit filed by the Forest Service claimed that the men had left hot embers in a campfire on July 26, the day the fire was first spotted. According to the complaint, they'd built the campfire within a ring of rocks in an area of dry twigs, pine needles and pine cones, and then left the area, "negligently failing to extinguish the campfire completely, to check the fire to ascertain whether it had been extinguished completely, and to take other precautions to prevent reignition of the fire." The federal government asked for $5,759,981 in damages from the three men to repay the cost of fighting the Mortar Creek fire.

How can Forest Service investigators pinpoint the exact

place where a wildland fire started after it has consumed tens of thousands of acres? They begin in the area where the fire was first reported, then piece together bits of evidence, which usually fit like a jigsaw puzzle. Forearmed with information about the burning conditions at the time of the fire—the weather, how strongly and in which direction the wind was blowing, the fuel buildup, their knowledge of fire behavior—they study char patterns in the burned-over area.

Fire generally moves in one direction. If it moves from north to south, for instance, the north side of trees will be burned more deeply than the south side. This causes trees to fall with their tops pointing north, just as trees being logged fall on the side from which a chunk has been cut. Grasses, too, fall pointing in the direction fires came from.

Pine needles and small twigs attached to trees or brush, on the other hand, are blown forward by the wind the fire generates. After they flash over and cool, they are still pointing in the direction the fire traveled.

Using these signs, which tell where a fire came from and where it went, investigators backtrack over the charred remains. They know when they're approaching the point of origin because a wildland fire is never as hot when it first starts as it becomes after it spreads. Since the fuels at the starting point haven't been completely consumed, it's possible to find the remains of campfires and even of burnt matches.

Fires caused by people are not part of the cycle of nature; they disrupt it. They cause the most damage because they start in areas people use most rather than in remote wilderness, where burning has less effect on land use. The new fire policy does *not* mean that people can be careless with fire, any more than they were a dozen years ago. Smokey Bear still urges all of us, "Please continue to be careful with fire."

# Jan Knight

## RANGE CONSERVATIONIST

$\mathcal{A}$lthough they're several million years old, Utah's Henry Mountains form one of the world's youngest mountain ranges. Some of the layers of sandstone thrust on edge by the earth's violent upheavals are bare and rugged, escalating in color from beige to bright orange. Others have been softly carpeted by the dull green of pinyon pines and junipers. Here and there miles-square patches of ground are littered by blackened, uprooted trees, with desert shrubs and grasses growing among the tree-skeletons. At first glance these patches look like the remains of wildland fires, but they're actually the result of "chaining." The trees were torn from the ground by a ship's anchor chain stretched between two big bulldozers so that the soil they stood on could be reseeded for better plant growth.

On a typical summer day, Jan Carol Knight kneels among the desert shrubs, clipping all the varieties of plant life in a 9.6-square-foot area. She separates the vegetation by type and puts each species into a brown paper bag, weighs the bag on a hand scale, and records the weight on a chart. Then she moves to another square and repeats the procedure. Jan's work will assure that all animals living in the Henry Mountains have enough of the right kind of food.

Summer is a favorite time of year for Jan, as it was during her childhood days in Whittier, California, when her father would take her to work with him. As an inspector for the Agricultural Commissioner's Office in Los Angeles County, Mr. Knight examined plants that came into California, making certain they were not hosts to pests that could damage the state's agriculture. Sometimes he brought Jan and her younger sister to a wholesale flower market in downtown Los Angeles. As Mr. Knight checked potted plants for pests, disease, or insects, the girls sniffed the spicy and sweet fragrance of newly cut blossoms, watching local florists choose the prettiest ones for their shops.

Another of Mr. Knight's duties, and the most interesting to blonde, green-eyed Jan, were the trap runs designed to find Japanese beetles and fruit flies. In Mr. Knight's area, thirty insect traps had been set up in people's yards. Jan looked on as her father sorted through the contents of each trap to discover whether any of the dreaded pests had slipped into the state.

Perhaps as a result of these early excursions with her father, Jan began to think about a career in natural resources by the time she reached her senior year in high school. It was 1973. All across the country, interest in conservation and ecology was high.

"I didn't have a very good idea of what kind of work it would be," Jan says. "I didn't know what those people did, really. From the high-school library I got the addresses of colleges that offered majors in the field and I wrote to a few of them, asking for their views about women in those professions."

When the replies began to reach her, Jan was most impressed by a letter from Thadis Box, the dean of the College of Natural Resources at Utah State University. He wrote:

*"As far as the kinds of jobs available for women are concerned, I am happy to report that the field has never been better for women than it is now. Many of the government agencies in particular are making a concerted effort to increase their number of women employees. I would like to think that by the time you graduate in one of the natural resource fields, employment and promotion will be geared primarily to a person's ability rather than to one's sex. I assure you that as far as I am concerned, if you make application for admission to Utah State University, you will get the same consideration as a male student."*

Jan learned that the field of natural resources is divided into several classifications. These include forestry; recreation planning; wildlife, watershed, and range management; and others. "Range management sounded best to me," she says. "It incorporated a little bit of everything I was interested in—botany, ecology, livestock management."

During the winter of her high school senior year, Jan was invited to take a scholarship examination at Utah State University. She flew to Logan, Utah, where the university campus sits high on a hill overlooking the town below. Hundreds of other scholarship aspirants had come from all over the country that weekend, one of them a girl from the state of Washington who would win the five-thousand-dollar award and become Jan's roommate the next year. On Saturday afternoon the high school students were invited to visit the departments that interested them.

"Quite a few of us walked to the natural resources building," Jan remembers, "but when it came time to split off into the individual departments, I was the only person who went to range science. All the others went to forestry or wildlife. I found myself all alone with the head of the range department, Don Dwyer."

At a first meeting, Jan's keen intelligence is obscured by her quiet, almost shy, personality. She couldn't think of a single question to ask Dr. Dwyer. "I guess I realized that I wasn't the traditional type of range prospect. If Dr. Dwyer hadn't been so accepting, I might have gone off somewhere else, where there were more kids. He told me about the department and the jobs which would be available to me if I majored in range."

Though Jan knew little about it at the time, 45 percent of the earth's land surface is classified as rangeland. It includes the tundra of Alaska, the steppes of Russia, the savanna and veld in Africa, the outback of Australia, and most deserts. In the United States, "range" describes such different kinds of land as the grassy Great Plains and the dry Mojave Desert. Range is land that is generally not suitable for agriculture or timber production, but can be grazed by wild and domestic animals.

When mankind first learned to domesticate animals, there seemed to be an unlimited supply of forage for cattle, sheep, goats, reindeer, and camels. If herds ate all the vegetation in a particular area, nomadic herdsmen moved their flocks to a new location, unconcerned about the barren ground they had left behind. More than a thousand years ago, after the mighty cedars of Lebanon had been cut to build ships and houses, no second growth of trees took their place because flocks of goats chewed the seedlings down to the roots. Even today in North Africa, animal herds overgraze the thin vegetation, turning grazing land into desert. Each year the earth's deserts increase by as many as 27,000 square miles.

At the end of the nineteenth and the beginning of the twentieth centuries in the United States, large numbers of homesteaders settled in the Great Plains region. They planted wheat, and fought gun battles with cattlemen who were already there driving steer and sheep over the vast, unfenced, open range. The settlers claimed that cattle's hoofs and appetites denuded the soil, which was true, but the farmers also exposed soil to wind erosion when they plowed up grass to make way for crops. In the 1930s, after several seasons of drought, the soil began to blow away in parts of Kansas, Oklahoma, Texas, New Mexico, and Colorado, so violently that clouds of dust darkened the sky as far away as the Atlantic coast. Thousands of families left the Dust Bowl to move west. These were the families John Steinbeck wrote about in *The Grapes of Wrath*.

The devastation of the Dust Bowl years led to the development of range management—ways to keep rangeland from turning into wasteland. By the 1940s, range management was an established science, and most western universities offered programs in range.

## THE BUREAU OF LAND MANAGEMENT

*W*hen Jan Knight declared range management as her major at the start of her freshman year at Utah State, there was only one other woman in the program, a senior. Toward the end of her first quarter Don Dwyer called Jan to his office. He told her that interviewers from the Bureau of Land Management were recruiting range students for a trainee program, and they would like to talk to her.

Jan was astonished. "I couldn't imagine why they wanted to talk to *me!* I didn't even have one quarter of college completed, and I hadn't yet taken any courses in range management. I didn't consider myself a very appealing job prospect for anyone."

But at that time, because of the Equal Employment Opportunity Act, federal agencies were being prodded to hire women and minorities. The Bureau of Land Management had a hard time finding "professional" women, women who were trained to do fieldwork rather than office work. Although Jan was just a freshman, she seemed certain that she wanted to work in range, she was doing well in her classes, and Don Dwyer spoke highly of her. The people from the BLM were anxious to meet her.

"When I went to the interview I was sort of nervous," Jan says, "so I don't remember much about what they asked me."

In spite of Jan's nervousness, the interviewers were impressed by her air of dependability and her interest in the profession. They told her to take a Civil Service test and to fill out a job application for the BLM. If she passed the test, the bureau would place her in a summer job each year until she graduated. Then, after she received her degree in range management, she'd be promoted to a professional position with the BLM.

Like most other Americans, Jan wasn't sure of just what the Bureau of Land Management did. Yet she was flattered that they wanted her, and she was eager to be hired by an agency that would help her to learn more about her future profession while she earned money during the summers.

The Bureau of Land Management, established in 1946 as a custodian of public lands, is one of the newer federal agencies. Public lands, comprising one fifth of the nation's total acreage, are what was left over after private individuals, corporations, state and local governments, and previously established federal agencies claimed the more desirable areas of the country. BLM territory is sometimes called "the land nobody wanted."

The 174 million acres in eleven western states and an additional 224 million acres in Alaska are "leftovers"—too cold and barren, or too dry for farming, or too rugged for settling, and hard to get to because the few roads that reach them are often impassable in winter. In pioneer times scattered ranchers grazed cattle and sheep on them and miners searched for gold or silver, but for the most part they were bypassed. They have always belonged to the federal government, acquired by the Louisiana Purchase, Indian treaties, and the war with Mexico. As described in a Department of Interior publication, "BLM lands stretch from the border of Mexico to the Arctic Ocean. They include desert and tundra, sagebrush and rain forests, mountain meadows and dry lakebeds whose aquatic life lies dormant, waiting for rain." And nobody wanted them. Until recently.

In fifty years America's population doubled. Since more people wanted to eat more beef, ranchers increased their herds to fill the demand. Cars and trucks needed the oil lying beneath BLM lands; factories wanted the coal. The once-sleepy towns of the Southwest mushroomed into metropolises that desperately needed water. And the people crowded into those metropolises wanted some wide open spaces where they could be alone, either to look at mountains and deserts or to race dune buggies and motorcycles. Suddenly everybody wanted "the land nobody wanted."

Environmentalists claimed that the territory should be kept

in a wilderness state, while private citizens clamored to increase grazing, mining, and water-use development. BLM policy had to change to meet new mandates from Congress, which reflected changing conditions; it now attempts to satisfy everyone's demands to a certain extent while protecting the land from exploitation. This is called "multiple-use planning."

In her first summer with the BLM, Jan examined erosion on the land around Price, Utah. For a month she went into the field each day with her supervisor, learning to estimate the degree of soil erosion on the desert floor and in the gray shale hills and mesas. Her supervisor also taught her to drive a four-wheel-drive stick-shift truck. Until then, Jan had always driven cars with automatic transmissions.

After that month Jan went out by herself each day, driving along deserted roads to the area she would survey. She was not afraid to work alone. "Once I got going, I wasn't very scared of anything," Jan recalls. "I never saw any scorpions or rattlesnakes, and I rarely saw any people. Sometimes there were situations in driving, though, where I wasn't sure what to do. That was the only thing that concerned me, that I'd do something stupid with the truck."

And of course, the thing she worried about most actually happened.

On a day in July, Jan was driving up a mountain road in an area shaded with juniper and pinyon trees. "I was in too high a gear and the truck started stalling before I reached the crest of the hill, so I decided I'd back down the incline, put it into a lower gear, and start all over again. Well, I wasn't watching where I was going when I backed the truck, and I got hung up on a big rock."

When Jan jumped out of the truck to look, she saw three wheels spinning in the air; only one front tire still touched the ground. She was 20 miles from the nearest town, on a

Jan has learned to drive her truck over rocky, muddy, washed-away roads.

road no one was likely to drive past for the rest of the day, maybe longer.

"I panicked," Jan says. "Not because I was scared, but because I was so mad at myself and terribly embarrassed that I might have to radio for help."

Jan got out the jack, thinking she could lift the truck and move the rock. For fifteen minutes she tried to figure out how to work the jack, but no one had taught her that. After she gave up on that idea, she stretched out on the ground to examine the rock, which was dead-centered beneath the truck. She thought she might be able to get enough traction from the one front wheel to "rock the rock." With a shovel she loosened soil around the 3-foot rock, then dug a hole in the soft, gravelly dirt behind it.

Starting the motor, Jan shifted the truck into forward and reverse again and again until the rock scooted backward

"There are still a few people
who think that a woman can't
do a good job in the field.
That strikes me as an
ignorant attitude, because
in my line of work there's
nothing a woman can't do."

into the hole. All four wheels touched the ground, and Jan
drove away.

Back in Price that night, she didn't mention what had happened to anyone. "I was the only woman working there that
summer, and I didn't want to listen to any cracks about
women drivers. There are still a few people who think
women can't do a good job in the field. That strikes me as
an ignorant attitude, because in my line of work there's
nothing a woman can't do. Physical strength is not an advantage unless your truck gets stuck somewhere, and even
then, if you use your brain, you can usually get out of it
okay."

The summer after her sophomore year Jan returned to Price, again working alone in the field. She did a little bit of erosion study, but mostly she studied the plant growth and composition on selected plots of ground. Her findings would be compared to records taken in earlier years. That way the BLM could tell whether certain weeds, shrubs, or trees were spreading in an area.

Jan got a change of scene that summer when she traveled by helicopter to the Green River, where she helped a wildlife specialist count deer droppings. Since wildlife experts know how many pellets a single deer will drop in one day, they can get an idea of the number of deer using an area by counting the pellets in a plot. The work was tedious, but the scenery—whitewater rapids splashing between rough sandstone cliffs—made it worthwhile.

By her junior year Jan was taking courses in range management: wildlife studies; livestock management and animal-science courses; and the basic uses of rangeland. That summer the BLM put her to work in the state office, compiling grazing records. She studied the appeals of ranchers who wanted to graze more cattle on BLM lands, and organized papers in cases where grazing privileges had been canceled. Jan learned a lot that summer, mostly that she'd rather be out doing fieldwork.

In June 1977, Jan graduated from Utah State University with a Bachelor of Science degree in range management. The BLM had guaranteed her a job after graduation, but Jan wasn't ready to go to work. "I was really burned out," she says. "I didn't want to go to school. I didn't want to go to work. I didn't want to do anything for a while. For four years I'd been away from home most of the time, taking classes nine months of the year and working every summer. I wanted a long vacation at home with my mother and dad and sister. When I got in touch with the Bureau of Land

Management and told them I'd rather not begin until the first of the year, they were understanding. They said, 'Okay, we'll have something for you then.' "

## THE HENRY MOUNTAINS

*E*arly-morning wind blowing through pin-yons and junipers makes a sound somewhat between a whistle and a howl. It blows Jan's straight blonde hair into her eyes. She brushes it back so that she can see in order to jot figures on the forms in her clipboard. She wishes she had an extra hand, because the wind is riffling the papers, too.

Early morning wind riffles hair and papers.

Pinyon and juniper make interesting patterns, but little forage grows beneath them.

Her partner, Pam Cordery, paces off the ground. Two steps make one pace; every two paces Pam describes what she finds beneath a notch in the toe of her boot. "Gravel, persistent litter," Pam says as Jan marks it down. Gravel is any piece of rock under 3 inches in size. Persistent litter does not mean trash left behind by determined campers; it refers to a surface layer of slightly decomposed leaves.

Standing in the same spot, Pam describes the growth from the ground up. She speaks in botanical shorthand, "*Pi ed, Am ut.*" *Pi ed* stands for *Pinus edulis,* the Latin name for pinyon pine, or piñon, as most dictionaries spell it. *Am ut* is *Amelanchier utahensis*. It would be easier but less specific to call it by its common name, serviceberry.

Pam continues walking in a straight line until she's gone twenty paces, having called out the ground cover and taller vegetation ten times. Where Pam stops, Jan comes to sample a "plot," putting down a marker made of three lengths of aluminum pipe joined at right angles to form an open-ended square. With hand shears, the girls clip every bit of vegetation in the plot down to the roots, afterward weighing each individual species. The gram-weights will later be converted to total production in pounds per acre for every type of plant in the area. When they've clipped ten of those plots in a straight line of two hundred paces, the girls will most likely have sampled everything growing on that ridge.

By the time they've finished a transect (ten plots or more) the sun soars high overhead. Jan peels off her down-filled parka. It is, after all, only late summer, although the tops of the Henry Mountains don't warm up until noon. Pam, a temporary employee, removes the peaked railroad cap that has held up her long brown braids. Then the girls climb into a truck and drive to a spot with a sweeping overlook of the Henrys, where they eat their lunches out of brown paper bags.

Driving after lunch to a new area where they'll work during the afternoon, they come upon part of the Henrys' herd of buffalo, grazing in a "chaining"—an area that has been chained and reseeded. Several bulls raise their massive heads to decide whether Jan and Pam are a threat to the herd. The buffalo cows and calves continue to graze on the relatively lush grass of the chaining.

In 1941, twenty-two buffalo—eight bulls, and fourteen cows—were transplanted from Yellowstone National Park to

The girls clip every bit of vegetation in a plot, then weigh it on a hand scale.

The area behind Jan has been chained and reseeded for better plant growth.

the Henry Mountains. Today the herd numbers close to two hundred, the only herd of free-roaming, hunted bison in the continental United States. Sometimes in the summer the big animals climb to the high peaks of the Henrys to forage— behavior considered quite untypical for buffalo, which are usually known as plains animals.

Much of the work Jan does is related to these buffalo. The

Bureau of Land Management permits privately owned cattle to graze in the Henry Mountains. Since buffalo and cattle eat the same kinds of grasses and shrubs, they compete with each other for existing food. If too many cattle are allowed

Sometimes in the summer these Henry Mountain buffalo climb to the high peaks to forage.

to graze on these public lands, there won't be enough food for the buffalo, and the reverse will be true if the buffalo herd grows too large. Jan's inventory gives the BLM a good idea of the amount of food available on 1½ million acres of the Henrys.

When the inventory is completed, the BLM will know how many cattle should be allowed to graze (one cow eats 800 pounds of feed in one month) so that both buffalo and cattle can thrive without harming the natural resources.

If cattle do not crop off grass too close to the roots, if they eat only the surface growth and move on to the other sections from month to month, the grass will grow again during the year. But if cattle (and buffalo) eat grass in the same area all year long and keep it too close-cropped, the grass can't build up the necessary carbohydrate reserves in its roots. Carbohydrate reserve is what the grass survives on in winter and what it needs to be able to sprout in the spring. When grass has no more green growth for photosynthesis to make food reserves to be stored in the roots, it will eventually die. Then sagebrush and other shrubs move in, and the land is no longer as desirable for grazing.

Cattle and buffalo aren't the only animals in the Henrys. Deer, antelope, coyotes, a few mountain lions, and elk range over the high peaks and the low desert, along with many smaller species, such as rabbits and ground squirrels. All sorts of reptiles and birds share the territory, too, but the smaller animals and birds can find enough to eat without threatening the well-being of the larger animals.

The deer herds in the Henrys exist in a cooperative balance with the cattle and buffalo, because although deer like to eat grasses in the spring, they can exist comfortably on shrubs that are not too attractive to the larger animals. Deer-grazing can even benefit cattle. When deer eat sagebrush, bitterbrush, cliff rose, mountain mahogany, and ser-

In the Henry Mountains, the deer and the antelope play—and compete for food with cattle, buffalo, and smaller species of wildlife.

viceberry, they keep these shrubs in check so that they don't spread over an area. Grass can then grow in greater abundance because it isn't competing with the shrubs.

As Jan marks down the plant growth on her form sheets, she classifies it by height, too, because sheep, cattle, antelope, and deer can reach different levels of leaves. For that reason, when BLM specialists compute the amount of food available to all kinds of animals on the range, they won't allot any growth over 7 feet tall to antelope, for instance. Antelope can't reach that high, although deer can when they stand on their hind legs.

In addition to classifying the plant growth by height, Jan records its stage of growth. Beginning growth, vegetation, bud, peak flower, seed ripe, mature, and dormant—these are the stages of plant growth. A plant provides most food at the "peak flower" stage, but it would be impossible for Jan and the nine other range conservationists on her crew to weigh and record each plant at just that time. They do, though, bring back specimens of all the plants at all stages to record their weights and various other measurements. With this information they can convert the figures on the forms to peak production weight.

Jan and Pam want to do another clipping in the high ridge area, but they choose a spot far enough away from the buffalo so that the herd won't become nervous and stampede. Here they put down a plot marker that looks like a hula hoop. A three-sided marker is used only where the hoop can't fit over trees or shrubs. They find eight different species of plants in this plot. One of them is a very tiny Antennaria, or "pussy toes." It takes the girls a lot of time to sift through the thick growth to find every single minuscule Antennaria before they can go on to the next seven species.

Three hours pass by the time all the vegetation in that plot has been sorted, weighed, and recorded. Jan and Pam stand up, rubbing their knees to ease the stiffness, then go on to finish the transect. It's well past five o'clock by the time they drive back to the cabin they share with two other range conservationists, or range cons, who are summer temporaries. Tonight the girls will be alone in the cabin. The temporaries are working the far side of the mountain and will spend the night with another crew in a BLM-owned trailer.

After they park the truck at the cabin, Jan takes an empty milk can and carries it to a nearby spring. Since the cabin doesn't have running water, the range cons get all their drinking, cooking, and washing water from the pure mountain spring. Pam helps Jan carry the can back to the cabin. It's so heavy that both girls strain to lug it up the porch steps.

Since the cabin doesn't have running water, Jan and Pam carry spring water inside.

Dinner is simple. They're too tired to fuss, and the kitchen cupboard doesn't offer much of a selection. It's Thursday, the time of week when the larder has grown bare. They'll replenish the food supply in Hanksville, Utah, the small town where the BLM office for the Henry Mountain area is located, and where the girls spend their weekends.

The sun is setting after Jan and Pam have washed the dishes and put them away. They sit on the porch steps to watch the always gratifying vista of rose-colored peaks and dusky pines. Fortunately, Jan and Pam enjoy each other's company. It can be pure misery to live twenty-four hours a day in almost total isolation with an uncongenial companion.

Darkness falls quickly in the Henrys. The girls go inside to light propane lanterns, preparing to spend a quiet evening reading and listening to music on a battery-powered tape recorder. Half an hour later a sweep of headlights shines through their uncurtained window. (Why put up curtains against prying eyes, when the nearest prying eyes are 40 miles away?)

Debbie, another temporary, who works on a farther part of the mountain, has come for a visit, bringing a paper sack full of pine cones. Jan rakes the coals in the wood-burning stove and puts in the pine cones to roast while the girls talk about their experiences during the past week. They gossip a bit about the love lives of all the other members of the crew. Most of them have come from out of state, leaving their boy friends and girl friends behind for the summer.

After a while Debbie reaches into the stove to pluck out, gingerly, one of the pine cones. Its scales have opened, and the pine nuts beneath are deliciously roasted. The girls dig

After dinner, Pam and Jan enjoy tea and talk until the sun sets.

out more pine cones and pull off the scales to get at the nuts, a slow and rather messy process that coats their fingers with soot and ashes. Pam makes hot lemonade from a canned mix, a perfect complement to the nuts.

"It's way after nine," Debbie realizes. "I don't think I want to make that thirty-mile drive back to my cabin on these roads. I'd probably go over a cliff in the dark. Anyway, I'm low on gas. Is it okay if I siphon some out of your truck in the morning? That is, if you don't mind me spending the night here."

Debbie goes out to her truck for a sleeping bag, then settles into one of the empty bunks as Jan turns out the lanterns and crawls into bed. The next day marks the end of the work week, when all the inventory crews will return to their quarters in Hanksville. Jan falls asleep, looking forward to a long shower and shampoo in a real bathroom in only twenty-four hours.

At four o'clock on Friday afternoon, Jan and Pam gather their dirty laundry, their grocery list, and the plant inventory forms and start the long drive back to Hanksville. Dust from the rutted, bumpy, razorback trail coats their truck, and the farther down the mountain they drive, the hotter it gets inside the truck cab. The girls would rather suffer from the heat, though, than open the windows to the dust.

The mountain terrain has changed to red desert country. Twice Jan gets out of the truck to open a ranch gate, closing it tightly after Pam has driven through. Although most of the wide Henry Mountain range is administered by the BLM, a few privately owned ranches occupy part of the land.

In less than two hours the girls are on paved road, a welcome change from the bone-jarring dirt trails. They drive through some of the most amazing scenery in the United States. Indians called it "the land of the sleeping rainbow." Towering orange rock is striated with buff-colored sandy lay-

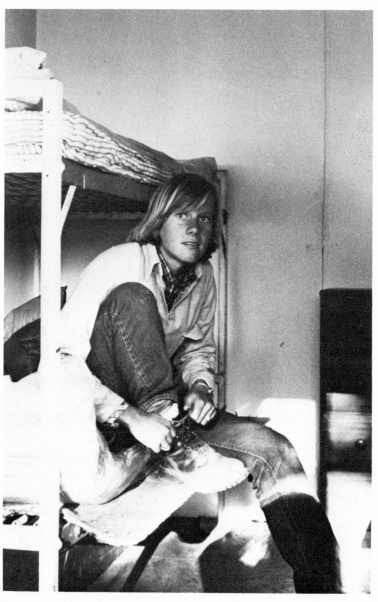

Jan gets ready for work as seven o'clock sunlight streams into the cabin.

ers and with purple and green bands of Morrison formation. It's in Morrison that rock hunters find fossilized dinosaur bone.

In the early part of the century, this territory was a hideout for some famous outlaws: Butch Cassidy and his Wild Bunch knew the trails, caves, and water holes well enough to shake off pursuing posses. Though Jan has seen this landscape a hundred times, she still appreciates the startling panorama.

At an intersection called Notom they turn onto Highway 24. Over the next few miles they pass rustic houses and much taller trees than the juniper and pinyon they're used to. Finally they turn off the road to the spot they've been anxious to reach, a small, ordinary-looking building marked "Cainville Trading Post." Their co-workers have gathered inside for companionship and the best Mexican food in Utah, a satisfying end to the work week in a job rich with satisfactions.

## MOBILITY

*B*y the end of October the vegetation in the Henry Mountains becomes dry and dormant. In November snow begins to fall, making the highest mountain roads impassable. For two winters Jan Knight returned to Richfield, Utah, to desk work, compiling all the inventory data collected over the summer months.

Range conservationists' work involves a sizable share of time behind a desk.

"People shouldn't go into range conservation thinking they'll always be outside roaming around the country," Jan says. "Range cons put in plenty of time behind a desk, too. I admit I sometimes found it tedious, putting together the figures for 300,000 acres, but there's a lot of important work that has to be done in the office."

Even while the information gathered during the previous summer was being processed into reports, plans were underway for the following summer's inventory. Range conservationists figured out in advance where they'd park their trailers in the field so that everyone could get to work in the shortest time. They ordered the supplies they would need: compasses, pencils, pens, dishes, forks, all the essentials for work and daily living. When spring once again crept over the Henrys, and the melting snow combined with spring rains to brush the barren land with fresh greenery and the startling color of desert flowers, Jan closed her desk and headed once again for the open.

Her job as a range conservationist has involved moving around quite a lot. In charge of quality control for the entire summer inventory, Jan traveled from camp to camp during her first two years in the Henrys, coordinating the activities of all the range crews and checking their paperwork and transect sites before resuming her own fieldwork. Each Friday afternoon she climbed into her truck for the bumpy ride back to Hanksville.

At Hanksville during those summer weekends, Jan lived in a one-bathroom government-owned trailer that she shared with seven other women working for the BLM. Each new season meant strange faces, a different group of temporary employees who would become good friends by the end of the summer and then go their separate ways.

"Lots of times, in this line of work, you have to live in small towns," Jan says, "often with people who have different values than you do, different ideas and life-styles. Some government career people don't like that, especially if they come from urban backgrounds. They feel a little alienated or uncomfortable."

This problem hasn't bothered Jan. Though she grew up close to the huge city of Los Angeles, she was able to adapt comfortably to small-town life, in Hanksville during the summers, and in Richfield for the winter routine of compiling reports.

In January 1980, Jan's paperwork was interrupted by an even farther move, to Phoenix, Arizona, for four months of classes at the Bureau of Land Management Training Center. Jan packed all her belongings once again into a U-Haul trailer, which she pulled behind her 1969 red Camaro. She drove across the desert, and unloaded everything into another temporary apartment.

After the fieldwork and the small towns, Phoenix was a decided change of pace. Tall, impressive buildings identified the downtown area. Flowers bloomed even in February, and palm fronds waved against the sky. Along with fifty other employees from several states, Jan sat in classes each weekday at the BLM Center, listening to lectures on public land policy. She was taught the laws and regulations of land management, and learned how to conduct herself in live courtroom situations. She might someday be called on to testify in a court case involving a land dispute.

Evenings and weekends were free for socializing, and Jan found herself surrounded by friends in a city where there was always a lot to do. "All of us wanted to make the most of the time we had together," Jan says, "because after the four months were over most of us would be going back to small-town living." They searched out unusual restaurants. They saw movies, played softball and volleyball, and went dancing a lot. Jan loved it. Some weekends they drove to the Mexican border, where Mexicans streamed across the checkpoint to buy American-made paper products and canned goods, while Jan and other Americans crossed to Nogales for handmade Mexican jewelry and embroidered blouses.

Other weekends they hiked and explored the Sonora Desert, a different kind of rangeland from the Henrys. "The Sonora was most beautiful in May," Jan remembers, "because that's when all the palos verdes were in bloom." "Palo verde" means green stick in Spanish, and that's what they look like, green bark with small green leaves and bright-yellow flowers. And there are octillo, with their 10-foot-tall stalks and reddish-orange blossoms on the tips that make them look like giant candles, and big saguaro cactus thrusting spiny arms into the sky. "The Sonora Desert is the kind of place most people think of when you say the word 'desert,' " Jan says. (The photograph of Jan on page 96 shows a saguaro and a palo verde.)

Moving around so much means extra work and constant adaptation, but Jan says, "I enjoy it quite a lot at this time of my life. I'm still a little apprehensive at first about meeting new people—that's just my personality—but in a very short time that feeling disappears when I get to know them. Later on, maybe, I'll want to settle down in one spot, but for a while I'd like to keep living this way."

After Phoenix, Jan returned to Hanksville to a slightly different job, which would require her to live in Hanksville year-round. She spent more time in the office, issuing grazing permits at the BLM rate, for 1980, of $2.36 per Animal Unit Month—what one cow and one calf can eat on the range in a month. This was quite a bargain compared to grazing fees on private property—$7.45 per AUM.

Her fieldwork includes vegetative inventory and use supervision: making sure that cattle are in the right place at the right time and in the proper numbers, checking that the wells and pipelines that provide water for the animals are working; and examining vegetation growth to decide when the cattle should be moved.

"A lot of my fieldwork is done on horseback," Jan says, "and that can be fun. Sometimes it's easier to count cattle on horseback, but other times they'll run more from a horse than a truck."

When any kind of private or government project is planned on BLM land, such as digging a gravel pit or erecting the transmission wires that stretch from pole to pole across almost every mile of rangeland, BLM staff people first examine the area to make sure that endangered plants won't be destroyed. They also look for Indian artifacts: fire pits, or agate chips, which show that Indians once made arrow-heads on that spot. The impact of a project on all multiple-use values—wildlife, watershed, recreation, range—is ana-lyzed, and if the impact would be serious, compromise measures are suggested by the BLM. Jan compiles informa-tion supplied by BLM specialists into impact reports that will be studied carefully.

In addition to Indian ruins and endangered plants, the Henry Mountain area offers vastly different types of terrain and points of interest that make it a hiker's paradise: sand dunes, hot springs, agate fields, and in a small grove of as-pen trees, a one-acre knoll known as "Nasty Flats."

Nasty Flats got its name from the obscene graffiti carved in the bark of its aspen trees. The words may have been carved by sheepherders stranded in the snow, who chose this way to express their disgust.

More pleasant graffiti is written on a 10,000-gallon water tank near the Big Thompson Mesa in the Henrys. It reads:

> *"In this parched area of the desert hem,*
> *The contents of this tank is a precious gem,*
> *With thirst on the brink*
> *Here is a drink,*
> *All compliments of our fine BLM."*

The verse is signed by a sheepherder from Hanksville, who evidently appreciates what the BLM is doing on the range-land.

If more Americans were aware of what the BLM has ac-complished, they too would be likely to approve. The bu-reau now has the legal responsibility, for the first time in history, according to Jan, to manage public lands for multi-ple use and sustained yield. "There's a need for dedicated resource managers," Jan says, "to apply their talents so that public land can continue to be used as its value is maintained and grows. There's great opportunity in this work, and a lot of challenge."

Cecil Andrus, who resigned as Secretary of the Interior in 1981, has said, "Unlike the huge private estates and hunting preserves of the rich and powerful, as in Europe and other regions of the world, our Federal lands are truly public. They are a legacy of freedom and openness for our children and grandchildren. They have contributed much to our people's feelings about what makes this country unique in the world."

# Land Use

## THE PEOPLE VERSUS THE PEOPLE

*T*he Bureau of Land Management, the U.S. Forest Service, the National Park Service, and all other federal agencies are divisions of the United States government. They were established by Congress. Their policies are decided by Congress. Since the people of the United States elect representatives to Congress, it follows that the federal agencies have grown out of the wishes of the people.

But the rules that control what people can or can't do on public lands often cause anger and rebelliousness. Just who is the boss? Who is the parent issuing orders? Is it the people or the government agencies? The situation is almost like a person getting mad at his or her own right hand for hurting.

Of the three resource agencies mentioned here, the National Park Service reaps the least criticism. Everyone enjoys the national parks, which give the American people superb recreation and unsurpassed scenery. People think of the Park Service as a benign big brother. Yet even the Park Service has come in for its share of hostility, as in a conflict that occurred in northern California a few years ago.

Redwoods are the world's tallest living things. The highest of them soars 370 feet into the northern California sky and is more than a thousand years old. A century ago 2 million acres of redwoods stood along the Northwest coastline, but today less than a sixth of them remain, the others having been cut down for their excellent building lumber.

To stay healthy, redwoods need a stable watershed around them. When too many trees surrounding a grove are cut away, the resulting erosion undermines the great trees and causes them to topple. To protect the giant trees, Congress established the 58,000-acre Redwood National Park in 1968.

Loggers protested against the park, saying it cost them jobs and income. Their opposition died down over the next decade, but flared again in 1977, when Phillip Burton of the U.S. House of Representatives proposed expanding Redwood National Park. Loggers had been cutting trees right up to the borders of the park, and erosion was threatening a grove containing the world's oldest and tallest redwoods.

Citizens of Humboldt County in northern California, who depended on logging for their incomes, were incensed by the proposed park expansion. When Representative Burton, who chaired the National Parks and Insular Affairs subcommittee in Congress, went to the city of Eureka to hold meetings on the expansion, local people filled the hall with shouts of protest, while others demonstrated against him in the streets outside.

For months bitterness ran rampant in Humboldt County as people denounced the Park Service, Representative Burton, President Carter, the Department of the Interior, and government in general. The bitterness didn't subside when Congress approved the park expansion in 1978. But job losses

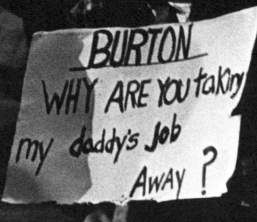

This girl's placard reflects the concerns of most people in Humboldt County over the expansion of Redwood National Park.

due to the expansion didn't hurt Humboldt County nearly as much as did the slump in the building industry over the next few years. The demand for redwood lumber fell drastically. As it turned out, people who had been put out of work by the 48,000-acre addition to Redwood National Park were better off than others, because the federal government offered them compensation pay and job-retraining.

While opposition to the National Park Service is relatively rare, the Forest Service is the target of a larger amount of criticism. The timber industry would like to see more commercial timber harvested from the national forests, while conservationists believe that old-growth stands of trees should be preserved for people to enjoy.

The let-burn policy concerning lightning-caused fires has also been criticized. Even while the Idaho fires of August 1979 were still burning, the state's governor, John Evans, flew over the charred acres and declared them to be in "the most serious condition that ever existed." He questioned the Forest Service decision to let the Gallagher Peak fire burn when it had seemed minor before the winds started to blow, saying, "The Forest Service did not recognize the serious fire conditions at that time. The fire should not have been allowed to go on as long as it did."

While the Park Service and the Forest Service cause controversy, the Bureau of Land Management is a whipping boy for a growing number of angry westerners.

Land is matter, the soil beneath our feet, the outer crust of the earth. It is inanimate. It cannot project emotion. But the feeling of ownership or of belonging to a particular segment of earth causes deep and fervent emotion in human beings: patriotism, possessiveness, pride, a sense of roots. We refer to the land as though it were alive—our Mother Earth; our country, God bless her; this is my own, my native land.

The love of land and the possession of it have created

passionate responses since prehistoric people first staked out their territories. Those same feelings are active in the Western states today, perhaps more intensely than in the East because the heritage of the West is newer. Cattlemen, ranchers, and residents of rural Western towns proudly retell the feats of their fathers and grandfathers, who opened the territory to homesteading, building roads and drilling wells. By virtue of that hard work, westerners feel that the land belongs to them.

But one-fifth of the total acreage in the United States, 354 million acres scattered through eleven Western states and Alaska, belongs to all United States citizens and is administered for them by the federal government. Until recently this land was managed by the Bureau of Land Management with little public attention or conflict.

In 1976, Congress passed the Federal Land Policy and Management Act. Before that year, people had assumed, if they bothered to think about it at all, that public lands would eventually be sold or transferred to private owners, or to the states where they were located. The new law clearly stated that all remaining lands would be owned by the federal government, forever, for the benefit and use of all the American people in all fifty states, unless disposal of a particular tract would be in the national interest.

That meant that large areas of the Western states would probably never belong, by title, to the local citizens: 66 percent of Utah, 86 percent of Nevada, 64 percent of Idaho, 60 percent of Alaska, and anywhere from one third to one half of California, Arizona, Colorado, Montana, New Mexico, Oregon, Washington, and Wyoming would be owned in perpetuity by the United States government.

Decades earlier, when these states had entered the Union, they'd agreed to give up all rights and titles to these lands, which had belonged to the federal government all along, in exchange for statehood. No one worried about it at the time, because the lands didn't seem to be worth much. In 1976, after the lands could no longer be acquired as they had in the past, people began to realize that they had value after all. And then they wanted to own them.

Many westerners felt they were being discriminated against. In the Eastern states, they argued, the federal government does not own and administer large tracts of land. This is true, because the Eastern states have been densely settled under private ownership for many generations.

Early in 1979, the Nevada legislature passed a bill challenging federal ownership of 50 million acres of Nevada territory, hoping to push the battle into the Supreme Court to force a test of federal land control. In June of that year California passed a similar bill. In Alaska, feelings ran so high that a small group of citizens talked about breaking away from the United States and forming a new country.

As this movement of discontent spread among westerners, it picked up the name "Sagebrush Rebellion." Not all westerners, by any means, supported the rebellion. Environmentalists and conservationists were delighted that so much land was going to be preserved in a natural state for the enjoyment of future generations.

Another thorn in the sides of the Sagebrush Rebels was the BLM's wilderness study. As part of the Federal Land Policy and Management Act, the BLM has been directed to study the wilderness potential of all roadless tracts of BLM land measuring 5,000 or more acres. If the areas have "outstanding opportunities for solitude or a primitive and unconfined type of recreation," if "the imprint of man's work is substantially unnoticeable," then that land is to be withheld from certain kinds of development or commercial use. Roads will not be cut through it. Motor vehicles will not be allowed on it, and people may enter the wilderness only on

# PUBLIC LANDS IN THE UNITED STATES

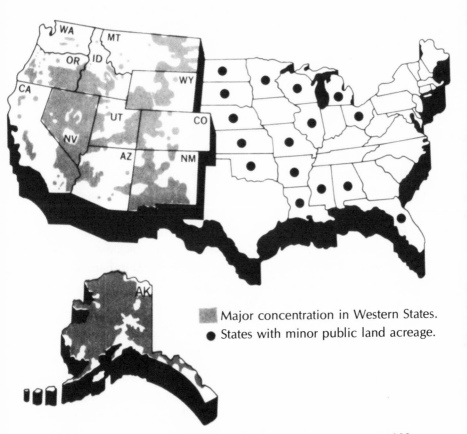

Major concentration in Western States.

● States with minor public land acreage.

| | | | |
|---|---|---|---|
| Alabama | 3,257 | Missouri | 200 |
| Alaska | 281,883,246 | Montana | 8,140,037 |
| Arizona | 12,595,821 | Nebraska | 8,581 |
| Arkansas | 1,589 | Nevada | 49,117,667 |
| California | 16,584,773 | New Mexico | 12,846,966 |
| Colorado | 7,996,260 | North Dakota | 68,142 |
| Florida | 1,189 | Ohio | 120 |
| Idaho | 11,949, 386 | Oklahoma | 7,112 |
| Illinois | 29 | Oregon | 15,724,455 |
| Kansas | 728 | South Dakota | 276,349 |
| Louisiana | 7,206 | Utah | 22,075,916 |
| Michigan | 936 | Washington | 310,239 |
| Minnesota | 43,556 | Wisconsin | 262 |
| Mississippi | 639 | Wyoming | 17,793,098 |

foot or horseback. Cattle-grazing will be allowed under strict controls, but mining, oil exploration, or other development will be permitted only if it does not impair wilderness characteristics of the land. The wilderness study is to be completed by 1991 or sooner.

This was good news to environmentalists, but states' rights supporters found the wilderness proposal a bitter pill to swallow.

The BLM invited people of all opinions to attend public meetings concerning each tract of proposed wilderness. If opponents could convince the BLM that these tracts were not suited to wilderness classification, the tracts would be dropped from the study.

In Hanksville, Utah, where Jan Knight's office is located, a public meeting was announced in May 1979. People were invited to speak their minds about a proposed wilderness area along the Dirty Devil River. Even though the area was under study, a uranium mining company called the Cotter Corporation had cut access roads across BLM land, some of them after the Federal Land Act was passed. If the area was set aside for wilderness study, the Cotter people would have to cover up the roads and restore them to a natural appearance, which they didn't want to do. Reclamation would take time and money, which Cotter preferred to spend on uranium exploration. Most of the local people were on Cotter's side, because the mining corporation provided jobs for them.

At the public meeting, which began at six thirty in the Hanksville School, more than one hundred twenty people filled the room, the majority of them residents from in and around Hanksville. Many had the stamp of the rugged land that had bred them, faces seamed from sun and weather, bodies hard and lean-muscled. A number of the men wore boots and Western hats; some of the women wore the elaborate hairdos favored in rural communities. The babies they cradled grew noisier as the meeting got underway.

One by one, people in the audience got up to express their opposition to the BLM, in voices strong with conviction.

"No reflection on you fellows [of the BLM staff]," said a man from a citizens' group to restore the Constitution. "You're just doing what Congress says. But dammit, Congress is wrong!"

Many people argued that the wilderness study would deny economic opportunity to the local residents. A speaker whose deep voice rose with pride declared, "We have at this time no welfare recipients in this county. None! We also have in this county not one draft dodger. Nobody ran to Canada when we went to Vietnam. These people have worked hard here; they've had very little. If they have an opportunity to have something, be it in this area or anywhere else, they're entitled to that opportunity. . . . These people are Americans, people who will give their all, and not rely on welfare or any other people to take care of them. What these people say in Wayne County, I think should be Gospel, because to me, that is America."

Loud cheers and applause echoed through the hall as the speaker took his seat.

After a number of wilderness opponents had expressed their views, an environmentalist took the floor. Of forty environmentalists who had made the trip to Hanksville, only two spoke at the meeting. Afterward they said that they'd been afraid to speak out because they were surrounded by hostile Sagebrush Rebels whispering pointed remarks.

"There are people other than backpackers," this man said, "who want this area designated a wilderness area. There are people in New York, all over the nation, that want these areas just for their own sake. They may never see them, but they know that maybe their children, some day, can come and visit them. . . . Those roads that were put in by Cotter Corporation last year were in direct violation of a piece of legislation coming down from Congress!" Although the previous speakers had sat down to resounding applause, this man's comments were followed by loud boos.

Later an elderly woman spoke about a visit she and her husband had received from "a nice young man from the Bureau of Land Management." She said, "We were feeling bad about the encroachment of our liberties in this country, and he became a little bit incensed, and he said, '. . . don't you know that there's a little old lady in a penthouse in New York that has just as much right to this land as you do?' And I said. . . . 'I wish I knew her, because I'd ask her, what difference does it make whether we call it a wilderness or not?' And she's just as welcome to come here as can be. Whether the Bureau of Land Management chooses to call it a wilderness area or what . . . it's still going to be just the way it is in the eyes of every one of us. It's our area. It's our land. It's our home."

The final comments came from a cattle grazer who announced, "What we need here is not a wilderness study. We need some BLM people to get off their butts and get out there and help administer with the tools that they've got. We don't need any more . . . laws! We need some cooperation among the multiple users. . . . The thing we object to is a bunch of damn schoolboys coming down here telling [us] how we're going to use our country that we beat our guts out to make!"

The above remarks are only a fraction of the speeches delivered during the two-hour meeting at Hanksville. It had been called by the Bureau of Land Management to learn the opinions of the people concerned with the Dirty Devil tract. Public meetings of this type were repeated in every section of Utah where federally controlled land had been proposed for wilderness study. As a result of people's comments and the Bureau's judgment, 20 million acres of land were released from the wilderness study, out of a total of 22,735,-168 acres of national resource lands under the jurisdiction of the BLM in Utah. The Bureau had asked for public input, and when the people spoke, the BLM listened.

As for the Dirty Devil area, the Bureau of Land Management filed a lawsuit to stop Cotter Corporation's plans to "blast, raze, level or construct" new roads through the area. Following a court decision in 1980, Cotter submitted a plan to reclaim and restore to a natural condition any roads that the company had built or would build. After some modification, the BLM approved the plan, which stated that within five years after it had first entered the land, Cotter Corporation would restore the access roads to a natural state and plant new vegetation to cover the soil, erasing all traces that the roads had ever been there. At this time, Cotter is working in the area.

In the first week of September 1979, a Sagebrush Rebellion "summit conference" took place in Reno, Nevada. Attorneys general, legislators, and county commissioners from ten Western states joined forces to plan a states' battle for federal lands. With Senator Orrin Hatch as the keynote speaker, the oratory became inflamed.

"I have come to you today," he said, "to ask you to join me in this second American revolution. If the Western states are ever to assume our rightful place, equal with other states of the Union, we must throw off the shackles in which the federal government now holds the destiny of the West."

He said that the government's disdain for property rights and decency has not been equaled since the first American Revolution threw out "the archetype of such oppression, pompous George the Third," and he asked, "Who is more thoughtlessly selfish than a cult of toadstool worshippers who unnecessarily lock up millions of acres of scenic beauty?"

The Reno conference ended with an expression of support for a bill Senator Hatch had introduced into the United States Senate. The bill would transfer title of public lands "to the state capital, and from there to county authorities, and ultimately, to private citizens." Although the bill seemed unlikely to be passed by Congress, its supporters gained new hope with the election of Ronald Reagan to the presidency. A self-proclaimed Sagebrush Rebel, Reagan said, "I renew my pledge to work toward a Sagebrush solution . . . to insure that the states have an equitable share of public lands and their natural resources." In one of President Reagan's most controversial appointments, James Watt succeeded Cecil Andrus as Secretary of the Interior. Environmentalists feared that Secretary Watt would permit overuse of public lands.

The Sagebrush Rebellion will probably continue to rage in the West for years, or even decades, as long as this basic question remains unresolved: Who morally and ethically owns these lands? The people as individuals, or the government of the people?

These public lands are administered by the national resource agencies, and the agencies are staffed with capable, high-caliber people who take their responsibilities seriously. Rangers, tourguides, naturalists, specialists, technical experts—all are dedicated professionals, anxious to share their areas with the real owners, the American people. Our public lands, and the men and increasing numbers of women who safeguard them, are truly a source of national pride.

# *Appendix*

## CAREER OPPORTUNITIES

*I*n addition to the jobs described in this book, the natural resource agencies offer a variety of other positions at the professional level. Since the federal hiring policy now demands equal employment opportunity for both sexes, and since fewer women than men have the educational backgrounds for these professional positions, the agencies welcome qualified women with enthusiasm.

During the beginning of the 1980s, however, federal hiring will probably be tight. Budgets have been trimmed in an economy drive; employees who leave their jobs are often not replaced. Young people who want to work for the national resource agencies should pay close attention to the advice of their college department advisors, who can inform them about the wisest selection of college courses for government jobs in the tough, competitive market.

According to a Forest Service personnel officer, "Certain

fields are easier to enter than others. For instance, job competition is keen in the field of forestry, but the Forest Service really needs civil engineers. And several Northwestern universities now offer degrees in forest engineering, which is geared to logging operations. Oregon State University in Corvallis has an excellent program in this field." The official adds, "A straight forestry degree nowadays is seldom enough. I recommend that students get dual degrees in forestry and something else, like wildlife, fisheries, range conservation, or business management, to increase their hiring potential."

College students who are looking forward to careers in the natural resource agencies may get an edge on the competition if they obtain temporary jobs with the agencies, as Karen Eckels did when she worked for the Youth Conservation Corps. This serves a dual purpose: the students become known to the program managers, and at the same time learn whether they really enjoy outdoor work enough to make it a lifetime career. After graduation, the temporary experience will be noted on their job applications.

Two federal programs also give students an advantage when they apply for federal jobs: one, the summer employment program for which Jan Knight was recruited; the other, a cooperative education program.

When the resource agencies learn that they're going to need professionals with specialized skills, they make formal agreements with universities for cooperative education programs. Job vacancy announcements are posted at the universities so that students can apply. The selected students work for the agencies for six months, and then return to college to finish their degree requirements. If they graduate with a 3.5 grade point average or better, the Bureau of Land Management does not require co-op students to take a competitive examination for a permanent position. Other agencies have somewhat different requisites.

The jobs young people consider most glamorous—park ranger and forest ranger—are the hardest to get. Less well known but vitally important positions can be easier to obtain if the applicant has the right background. Most of these positions tend to overlap in the three main natural resource agencies, the National Park Service, the U.S. Forest Service, and the Bureau of Land Management. Wildlife biologists, for example, are employed by all three agencies.

Listed below are several of the professional opportunities in the resource management field:

WILDLIFE BIOLOGY: Wildlife biologists are authorities on animals and fish. They're responsible for the protection of game and for the habitat management of rare and endangered species. The wildlife specialist should have a bachelor's degree or higher in biological science, with courses in plant and animal ecology, zoology, and botany.

ECOLOGY: Ecology is often called the interrelationship of nature. Ecologists deal with such matters as changes in plants and animals, including humans, and the structure and function of ecosystems. The ecologist should have a bachelor's degree or higher in plant and animal ecology, with some background in wildlife, forestry, range management, or environmental health science.

LAND CLASSIFICATION—REALTY: Realty specialists investigate the land, the environment, and the economy, and make recommendations on the proper use of public lands. Their educational backgrounds may be in land-use planning, agricultural economics, range management, forestry, mining engineering, geography, or geology.

PLANNING: Professionals in the planning program create multiple-use management plans to protect lands, resources, and environmental values from destruction. Educational background may include biological sciences, agriculture, natural resource management, geography, economics, or regional planning.

SURVEYING: A cadastral surveyor confirms boundaries in original surveys, some of them a hundred years old, and reestablishes boundaries in new surveys. Locating old boundary markers can be as tricky and challenging as finding buried treasure. Requirements are one to three years of surveying education plus work experience in surveying.

SURFACE PROTECTION: Surface protection specialists make sure the land is returned to a natural condition after a right of way is put through, or after mining is concluded on public lands, so that the ground won't be left in a scarred condition. Their backgrounds may be in mining or related subjects, biological science, mineral development, or reclamation.

RECREATION: Recreation specialists help meet the expanding needs of people for leisure-time outdoor activities while they protect the natural resources that make such leisure possible. They have degrees in resource management, landscape architecture, forest recreation, park management, or regional planning.

CONSERVATION: Conservationists deal with nonrenewable resources (coal, oil, minerals) and renewable resources (trees, grass, animals, water). They're involved with surveys, land and water management, habitat improvement, and research. Degrees in biological sciences or natural resources are required.

GEOLOGY: Geologists study groundwater conditions for watershed management; foundation conditions for road-building; soil stability; and the composition of landforms. They must have a degree in geology or one of its specialties: engineering geology, mining geology, or groundwater geology.

HYDROLOGY: Hydrologists are concerned with water resources. They analyze watershed conditions to prevent flooding and erosion, and to assure a continuous supply of fresh, clean water on public lands. Their degrees should be in watershed management, hydrology, or aquatic biology.

LANDSCAPE ARCHITECTURE: These specialists design outdoor recreation facilities and improvements that must not interfere with the natural appearance of public lands. They supervise construction, and work in cooperation with community planning agencies and public officials. Required is a bachelor's degree in landscape architecture or design.

SOIL SCIENCE: A knowledge of soils is essential to all phases of multiple-use planning. The soil scientist determines what plants will grow in an area, how much rainwater will be stored in the soil, whether the land can be grazed, and the dangers of erosion. Most of these specialists have degrees in soil science, but some have degrees in forestry, agronomy, range management, or geology.

WILDLIFE REFUGE: Wildlife refuge managers develop management and operational plans for bird and game refuges, see that wildlife is properly protected, and work with individuals and organizations in maintaining wildlife sanctuaries. They need degrees in wildlife biology or zoology.

ARCHAEOLOGY: Archaeologists research historic and prehistoric cultures, predominantly those of the American Indian. They find and preserve artifacts, putting together exhibits about ancient peoples who inhabited the public lands. Their degrees in archaeology must include twenty semester hours of anthropology.

HISTORY: At national historic sites, historians research the importance of the sites to the American people, and write interpretive programs. The position requires a degree in history or experience in political science, international law, or international relations.

This is a sampling of resource jobs available at the professional level. It is possible, though difficult, to obtain these professional positions without a college degree, substituting undergraduate college courses combined with work experience in the field. However, so many applicants *with* degrees apply that the positions are almost always filled by college graduates.

Below the professional level, jobs are available for aides and technicians. In the National Park Service, these non-professionals perform many of the basic day-to-day operations in the parks. Technicians may guide visitors along well-marked trails. They give guide talks that have been written by the rangers. Because budget cuts have reduced the number of available rangers, many qualified technicians perform ranger-level duties, gaining excellent opportunities to work into full ranger positions when they become available.

Park aides are trainees who receive on-the-job experience. They may operate campgrounds, restock firewood, collect fees at entrance stations, and give guided tours under the supervision of a ranger or a technician. Aides must have one or two years of college, technicians two or more years.

Park Service aides and technicians are not required to take a government test before being hired. Instead, they fill out a form that lists their college level and practical work experience. After the form is scored by a computer, a list of the highest scorers goes out to the various parks.

In the Forest Service, nonprofessional employees plant trees, work on flood control, disease and insect control, and construction. Technicians may supervise a road-building crew or an on-the-ground operation in timber sales. Aids may scale logs, mark trees, record soil moisture, or work on road crews.

With the Bureau of Land Management, aides and technicians work under crew leaders supervising the various jobs, such as inventory control and land reclamation. Nonprofessionals in the BLM are generally summer temporary employees, rarely full-time.

As long as the job situation remains tight, the best way to work into a professional position with the natural resource agencies will be through a summer employment program, a college co-op program, or a job as an aide or technician. Many federal agencies other than the three mentioned here offer similar resource positions, although they don't hire as many employees. According to Robert K. Walker, information officer in the Office of the Secretary, Department of the Interior, "The Fish and Wildlife Service and the Water and Power Resources Service in the Department of the Interior; the Corps of Engineers, and National Marine Fisheries in the Department of Commerce also have responsibilities for resources management. And, because these agencies aren't so well known, the competition for the jobs might not be as tough." Information about them can be obtained through the Federal Job Information Centers in major metropolitan areas throughout the country.

State agencies also offer resource positions.

# DEGREES OFFERED IN PARK ADMINISTRATION

*T*his partial list was drawn from information supplied by the Society of Park and Recreation Educators, a branch of the National Recreation and Park Association, 1601 North Kent Street, Arlington, Virginia 22209. The association may be contacted for further information.

Arkansas Technical University
Department of Recreation and
  Park Administration
Russellville, Arkansas 72801

California State Polytechnic
  University, Pomona
3801 West Temple Avenue
Pomona, California 91768

Illinois State University
Recreation and Park
  Administration
McCormick Hall
Normal, Illinois 61761

Western Illinois University
Department of Recreation and
  Park Administration
103 Western Hall
Macomb, Illinois 61455

Indiana University at Bloomington
Department of Recreation and
  Park Administration
School of Health, Physical
  Education and Recreation
Bloomington, Indiana 47405

Eastern Kentucky University
Department of Recreation and
  Park Administration
Richmond, Kentucky 40475

University of Kentucky
Department of Health, Physical
  Education and Recreation
100 Seaton Building
Lexington, Kentucky 40506

Western Kentucky University
Department of Physical Education
  and Recreation
Bowling Green, Kentucky 42101

Central Michigan University
Department of Recreation and
  Park Administration
Mount Pleasant, Michigan 48859

Michigan State University
Department of Park and
  Recreation Resources
131 Natural Resources Building
East Lansing, Michigan 48824

University of Minnesota, at
  Minneapolis
Division of Recreation, Park and
  Leisure Studies
203 Cooke Hall
1900 University Avenue Southeast
Minneapolis, Minnesota 55455

University of Missouri, Columbia
Department of Recreation and
  Park Administration
624 Clark Hall
Columbia, Missouri 65211

University of New Hampshire
Recreation and Parks
227 Hewitt Hall
Durham, New Hampshire 03824

Ohio State University
Parks and Recreation
  Administration
2080 Neil Avenue
Columbus, Ohio 43210

University of Oregon
Department of Recreation and
  Park Management
Eugene, Oregon 97403

Pennsylvania State University
Recreation and Parks Program
267 Recreation Building
University Park, Pennsylvania
  16802

Clemson University
Department of Recreation and
  Park Administration
263 FRR Building
Clemson, South Carolina 29631

University of Tennessee at Martin
Park and Recreation
  Administration
Martin, Tennessee 38238

Memphis State University
Department of Park Administration
Memphis, Tennessee 38152

Texas A & M University
Department of Recreation and
  Parks
College Station, Texas 77843

Texas Technical University
Department of Park Administration
Lubbock, Texas 79409

Washington State University
Recreation Program
Smith Gymnasium 101
Pullman, Washington 99164

Shepherd College
Park Administration
Shepherdstown, West Virginia
  25443

---

# DEGREES OFFERED IN FORESTRY

---

$\mathcal{T}$his list was provided by the Society of American Foresters, 5400 Grosvenor Lane, Washington, D.C. 20014.

Auburn University
Department of Forestry
Auburn, Alabama 36830

Northern Arizona University
School of Forestry
Flagstaff, Arizona 86011

University of California
Department of Forestry and
  Resource Management
Berkeley, California 94720

Humboldt State University
School of Natural Resources
Arcata, California 95521

Colorado State University
College of Forestry and Natural
  Resources
Fort Collins, Colorado 80523

Yale University
School of Forestry and
  Environmental Studies
New Haven, Connecticut 06511

University of Florida
School of Forest Resources and
  Conservation
Gainesville, Florida 32611

University of Georgia
School of Forest Resources
Athens, Georgia 30602

University of Idaho
College of Forestry
Wildlife and Range Sciences
Moscow, Idaho 83843

University of Illinois
Department of Forestry
Urbana, Illinois 61801

Southern Illinois University
Department of Forestry
Carbondale, Illinois 62901

Purdue University
Department of Forestry and
    Natural Resources
Lafayette, Indiana 47907

Iowa State University of Science
    and Technology
Department of Forestry
Ames, Iowa 50011

University of Kentucky
Department of Forestry
Lexington, Kentucky 40546

Louisiana State University
School of Forestry and Wildlife
    Management
Baton Rouge, Louisiana 70803

University of Maine at Orono
School of Forest Resources
Orono, Maine 04469

University of Massachusetts—
    Amherst
Department of Forestry and
    Wildlife Management
Amherst, Massachusetts 01002

Michigan State University
Department of Forestry
East Lansing, Michigan 48824

Michigan Technological University
School of Forestry and Wood
    Products
Houghton, Michigan 49931

University of Michigan
School of Natural Resources
Ann Arbor, Michigan 48109

University of Minnesota at
    Minneapolis St. Paul
College of Forestry
St. Paul, Minnesota 55108

Mississippi State University
School of Forest Resources
Mississippi State, Mississippi
    39762

University of Missouri
School of Forestry, Fisheries and
    Wildlife
Columbia, Missouri 65211

University of Montana
School of Forestry
Missoula, Montana 59801

University of New Hampshire
Institute of Natural and
    Environmental Resources
Durham, New Hampshire 03824

SUNY College of Environmental
    Science and Forestry
School of Forestry
Syracuse, New York 13210

Duke University
School of Forestry and
  Environmental Studies
Durham, North Carolina 27706


North Carolina State University
School of Forest Resources
Raleigh, North Carolina 27650


Oklahoma State University of
  Agricultural and Applied Science
Department of Forestry
Stillwater, Oklahoma 74074


Oregon State University
School of Forestry
Corvallis, Oregon 97331


Pennsylvania State University
School of Forest Resources
University Park, Pennsylvania
  16802


Clemson University
College of Forest and Recreation
  Resources
Clemson, South Carolina 29631


University of Tennessee at
  Knoxville
Department of Forestry, Wildlife &
  Fisheries
Knoxville, Tennessee 37901


Stephen F. Austin State University
School of Forestry
Nacogdoches, Texas 75961

Texas A & M University
Department of Forest Science
College Station, Texas 77843


Utah State University
College of Natural Resources
Logan, Utah 84321


University of Vermont
School of Natural Resources
Burlington, Vermont 05405


Virginia Polytechnic Institute and
  State University
School of Forestry and Wildlife
  Resources
Blacksburg, Virginia 24061


Washington State University
Department of Forestry and Range
  Management
Pullman, Washington 99163


University of Washington
College of Forest Resources
Seattle, Washington 98195


West Virginia University
Division of Forestry
Morgantown, West Virginia 26506


University of Wisconsin, Madison
Department of Forestry
Madison, Wisconsin 53706


University of Wisconsin, Stevens
  Point
College of Natural Resources
Stevens Point, Wisconsin 54481

---

# DEGREES OFFERED IN RANGE MANAGEMENT

---

$\mathcal{T}$his list was provided by the Society for Range Management, 2760 West Fifth Avenue, Denver, Colorado 80204

Range Management Program
School of Renewable Natural
    Resources
University of Arizona
Tucson, Arizona 85721

Department of Botany and Range
    Science
Brigham Young University
Provo, Utah 85601

Department of Forestry and
    Conservation
University of California
Berkeley, California 94720

Department of Agronomy and
    Range Science
University of California
Davis, California 95616

Range Science Department
College of Forestry and Natural
    Resources
Colorado State University
Fort Collins, Colorado 80523

School of Forest Resources and
    Conservation
University of Florida
Gainesville, Florida 32601

Department of Range Management
School of Natural Resources
Humboldt State University
Arcata, California 95521

Range Management Section
College of Forestry, Wildlife and
    Range Sciences
University of Idaho
Moscow, Idaho 83843

Department of Animal and Range
    Sciences
Montana State University
Bozeman, Montana 59715

Department of Animal, Range and
    Wildlife Sciences
New Mexico State University
Las Cruces, New Mexico 88003

Rangeland Resources
Oregon State University
Corvallis, Oregon 97331

Animal Science Department
South Dakota State University
Brookings, South Dakota 57006

Department of Range Science
Texas A and M University
College Station, Texas 77843

Department of Range and Wildlife
    Management
Texas Technical University
Lubbock, Texas 79409

Range Science Department
College of Natural Resources
Utah State University
Logan, Utah 84321

Department of Forestry & Range
    Management
Washington State University
Pullman, Washington 99163

Range Management Section
Plant Science Division
University of Wyoming
University Station, Box 3354
Laramie, Wyoming 82070

## PAMPHLETS ON CAREERS

*T*hese pamphlets on careers in the natural resource field may be requested from the following organizations:

| PAMPHLET | ORGANIZATION |
|---|---|
| *Service to Humanity* | National Recreation and Park Association |
| *Careers in Parks, Recreation and Leisure Studies* | 1601 North Kent Street Arlington, Virginia 22209 |

| | |
|---|---|
| *Occupational Guide #232: Park Ranger* | California State Department of Employment<br>800 Capitol Mall<br>Sacramento, California 95814 |
| *Ask Any Forester* | Wild Acres<br>5400 Grosvenor Lane<br>Washington, D.C. 20014 |
| *Forest Ecology and You* | Society of American Foresters<br>1010 16th Street N.W. |
| *Forestry as a Profession* | Washington, D.C. 20036 |
| *The Work and Education of a Forest Manager* | State University of New York<br>College of Forestry<br>Syracuse, New York 13210 |
| *Occupational Guide #334: Fire Fighter—Forest* | California State Department of Employment<br>800 Capitol Mall<br>Sacramento, California 95814 |
| *Career Choices—Working Toward a Better Environment* | U.S. Environmental Protection Agency<br>Office of Public Relations<br>Washington, D.C. 20460 |
| *A Wildlife Conservation Career for You* | The Wildlife Society<br>3900 Wisconsin Avenue N.W.<br>Washington, D.C. 20016 |
| *Conservation Careers* | National Wildlife Federation<br>1412 16th Street N.W.<br>Washington, D.C. 20036 |
| *Your Career in Ecology* | Ecological Society of America<br>Department of Biology<br>Rutgers University<br>Camden, New Jersey 08102 |

## SOURCES OF INFORMATION

*T*he following agencies will answer questions and provide information on the subjects listed:

| SUBJECT | AGENCY |
|---|---|
| animals | Smithsonian Institution |
| educational programs | Office of Education |
| environmental protection | National Museum of Natural |
| historic preservation | History |
| wildlife | Tenth Street and Constitution |
| | Avenue, N.W. |
| | Washington, D.C. 20560 |
| | |
| environmental protection | Assistant Director, Public Affairs |
| recreation | United States Fish and Wildlife |
| water, waterways | Service |
| wildlife | Department of the Interior |
| | Washington, D.C. 20240 |
| | |
| environmental protection | Public Affairs Office |
| historic preservation | National Park Service |
| parks | Department of the Interior |
| recreation | Washington, D.C. 20240 |
| | |
| range | Office of Public Affairs |
| public lands | Bureau of Land Management |
| | Department of the Interior |
| | Washington, D.C. 20240 |

parks
forests
recreation
water, waterways
wildlife

Division of Personnel and
    Management
Bureau of Outdoor Recreation
Department of the Interior
Washington, D.C. 20240

environmental protection
recreation
water, waterways
wildlife

Office of Public Affairs
Bureau of Reclamation
Department of the Interior
Washington, D.C. 20240

conservation
environmental protection
fire protection
forest fire management
recreation
wildlife

Information Officer
U.S. Forest Service
Department of Agriculture
Washington, D.C. 20250

# *Index*